*Old Truths
for a New Day*

Old Truths for a New Day

❖ ❖ ❖

A SELECTION OF SERMONS
FOR THE FIRST HALF OF THE
CHURCH YEAR BASED ON TEXTS
TAKEN FROM THE EPISTLES BY

O. A. Geiseman, S. T. D.

PASTOR OF GRACE LUTHERAN CHURCH
RIVER FOREST, ILLINOIS

CONCORDIA PUBLISHING HOUSE
SAINT LOUIS, MISSOURI, 1949

DEDICATION

❖   ❖   ❖

To the men of Grace Church
whose co-operation makes possible the ever-widening out-reach
of a Gospel ministry.

Preface

♦

Once again it is my privilege, with the gracious co-operation of the publisher, to present in printed form a series of sermons which constitute one year of preaching. It is planned to have them appear in two volumes, of which this is the first. This volume contains the messages which were delivered from the First Sunday in Advent up to and including Easter Sunday.

If my observations are correct, then there has been only a limited amount of sermonic material published on the Old Line Epistles. Because of their rich Gospel content and because of their immediate practical significance for contemporary life, these texts certainly merit frequent pulpit treatment. Since many of the several hundred pastors who have read these sermons on the Epistle texts in mimeographed form have volunteered gracious and favorable comment, it is hoped by the publisher and myself that they might, under God, prove to be a helpful addition to the materials now available on the Epistles.

The reader will, of course, discover that for the sermons on Christmas Day and on Easter Sunday the Epistles appointed for those days were omitted in favor of texts (Luke 2:1-14, I Corinthians 15:12-20) which seem to be more clearly and directly applicable.

God granting grace, Volume II, which will contain sermons for the chief holy days and Sundays following Easter to the close of the church year, will appear at an early date.

THE AUTHOR

Grace Lutheran Church
River Forest, Illinois

Contents

◆

Christians, Wake Up!   1
(First Sunday in Advent) Romans 13:11-14

There Is Hope   11
(Second Sunday in Advent) Romans 15:4-13

How to Be Strong, Decisive, Victorious   22
(Third Sunday in Advent) I Corinthians 4:1-5

How to Be Happy   33
(Fourth Sunday in Advent) Philippians 4:4-7

God's Greatest Gift to Man   43
(Christmas) Luke 2:1-14

The Meaning of Christmas   53
(Sunday after Christmas) Galatians 4:1-7

A Cheerful Outlook   65
(New Year's Day) Galatians 3:23-29

Is Christianity Worth the Price?   76
(Sunday after New Year) I Peter 4:12-19

Light! Let It Shine!   87
(Epiphany) Isaiah 60:1-12

God's Plea   99
(First Sunday after Epiphany) Romans 12:1-5

A True, Living Church   109
(Second Sunday after Epiphany) Romans 12:6-16

How to Overcome Evil   122
(Third Sunday after Epiphany) Romans 12:17-21

Are You Winning the Race of Life?   130
(Septuagesima) I Corinthians 9:24–10:5

God's Grace Is Sufficient   139
(Sexagesima) II Corinthians 11:19–12:9

The Greatest of These Is Love   152
(Quinquagesima) I Corinthians 13:1-13

Receive Not . . . in Vain   162
(Invocavit, First Sunday in Lent) II Corinthians 6:1-10

A Principle and Its Application   173
(Reminiscere, Second Sunday in Lent) I Thessalonians 4:1-7

Children of Light   185
(Oculi, Third Sunday in Lent) Ephesians 5:1-9

Two Kinds of Religion   195
(Laetare, Fourth Sunday in Lent) Galatians 4:21-31

For Life and for Death   206
(Judica, Fifth Sunday in Lent) Hebrews 9:11-15

The Christian Faith   216
(Palm Sunday, Sixth Sunday in Lent) Philippians 2:5-11

Jesus Is Risen   228
(Easter) I Corinthians 15:12-20

*Old Truths
for a New Day*

Christians, Wake Up!

❖   ❖   ❖

*And that, knowing the time, that now it is high time to awake out of sleep; for now is our salvation nearer than when we believed. The night is far spent, the day is at hand. Let us therefore cast off the works of darkness, and let us put on the armor of light. Let us walk honestly, as in the day; not in rioting and drunkenness, not in chambering and wantonness, not in strife and envying. But put ye on the Lord Jesus Christ, and make not provision for the flesh to fulfill the lusts thereof.—*Romans 13:11-14.

If the Spirit of God will let me bring to you the message contained in the words of our text as it should be brought, then you will be a more wide-awake and a more alert Christian than you have been in the past. These words are designed to arouse us so that we will bestir ourselves to a finer kind of Christianity and a fuller measure of spiritual, moral living. Paul said to the Christians at Rome, "Awake." That exhortation needs to be addressed to us as well.

WE NEED THIS EXHORTATION BECAUSE WE ARE ASLEEP

It is right, I think, to say that one of the greatest though perhaps least recognized tragedies of our day is *the fact that*

1

Christians, professed sons and daughters of God, are half asleep, if not altogether asleep. This sleepiness and weariness, this want of alertness on the part of God's children, manifests itself in various ways. *It is to be seen in our want of spiritual understanding, in our failure properly to analyze the meaning of what is happening all around us in our everyday lives.*

If I were to ask this Christian audience, or any other Christian audience, why did we become involved in the Second World War, which was started thousands of miles away from here, I am afraid a great many folk would resort to some political answer. They would find the solution in some political analysis of the situation. They would not be conscious that wars are a scourge of God and that people who do not live in God's way will be called by Him from their erroneous ways to the right way even though it must be by war.

If I were to ask you why we have so much juvenile delinquency in our country, what would you say? Perhaps some of you would say that it is the result of the war. So many mothers went to work. So many children were neglected, and so we are getting all this behavior. Oh, I would not deny that that is a factor in the matter, but certainly that is not the real reason for it. The real reason for it is that the children's spiritual and moral training has been neglected. It was not boys and girls who were six, eight, ten, twelve years of age who needed the attention of their fathers and mothers who have caused so much trouble, but it was the older boys and girls, sixteen, seventeen, and eighteen years of age, who should have known how to behave themselves but who didn't. We Christians certainly ought to understand why these things are happening, but we don't. We are asleep. We are not applying Christian understanding to the ways of life and to an analysis of human conflict.

Recently I received a questionnaire from the head of a
Jesuit group of social students asking me to send them a
500-word answer to the question "What in your opinion are
the chief economic and social causes of the present-day
breakdown of the American home?" Well, it would not be
difficult to enumerate certain factors in the economic and
social conditions of our day contributing to this particular
and very serious problem in American life. But when you
look at that problem through the eyes of a Christian, in the
final analysis it is not an economic problem. The reason why
there is such a widespread breakdown of the basic institution
in human life is that so many people have lost their regard
for the binding quality of the holy bond of marriage. Others
may not understand that, but you and I as Christians should
be awake to the fact, and we should understand. ·

If I asked you: "Why were we so haunted and tormented
by a coal miners' strike within recent weeks? Why was the
dark cloud of gloom spread all over our country by this
uprising, as it were, in the world of American labor?" a great
many folk in the Church no doubt would be immediately
ready to say: "That was due to the irresponsible behavior of
John L. Lewis. He had some political ambitions. He wanted
to square an account, or he wanted to get ahead of other
labor leaders." Certainly, I am not going to deny that such
factors may have played into the situation, but you and I
are not wide-awake Christians if we think that this is the real
answer. No, this is only a part of the general picture in
American life. Why are we so far behind with our production? Why has our production not measured up to our antici-
pations? Why aren't we as prosperous as we have every
opportunity of being? Because a few people do not use good
sense? Oh, no! The meanings of life go much deeper than

that. God is talking to us. God is saying through a coal strike which can paralyze all American life and industry, our whole economic system, that we are not as strong as we think we are. Our whole structure of life is a very fragile thing. One coal strike can ruin us and overthrow our whole democratic system. One coal strike can throw us from a democracy into a Fascist dictatorship. Wake up! Don't be sleepy-eyed Christians who don't understand what is going on around you. Understand things in the light of spiritual and moral meaning and truth.

EXHORTATION IS NEEDED BECAUSE TIME SPEEDS ON

Then this admonition "wake up" is so important also because we let the hands on the clock of time go around and around and around, and act as though we had an eternity in which to accomplish the things that need to be done. Today men's souls are being lost. Today men are going away from the pathways which God has outlined for them and destroying themselves eternally. It is today that humanity has its problems. It is today that boys and girls are growing up before our very eyes who must either be fashioned into God-fearing men and women now or never become such. It is today that the hungry, empty stomachs of individuals are crying out for charitable help. It is today that people are naked and cold and homeless and without hope. Today you have the opportunity of growing into something finer. I do not know when you first came to believe in Jesus as your Savior, when you first said that you were a child of God and a disciple of Christ, but I do know that today you are closer to meeting your God either because He calls you to Himself or because He comes to judge the world in righteousness than you were when you first began to believe. Time is fleet-

ing. The clock does not stand still. It goes on. You and I have
one life to live. Yesterday will never come again. You see,
that is why it is so tragic that we as professed Christians
twiddle our thumbs and let time go by without doing anything about the needs and wrongs in the world, either by the
improvement of our own spiritual lives or by the improvement of life in society at large.

WHAT TO DO: PUT ON JESUS

Paul had a great sense of the urgency of time. That is why
he said: "The night is far spent, the day is at hand." Now is
the time to wake up and do something. Well, what should
we do? The Apostle tells us. *First,* he says, *"Put ye on the
Lord Jesus Christ."* We don't get anywhere at all in spiritual
matters until we do that. This is to be taken seriously. Some
of you who are here this morning may never yet have even
professed to have put on Christ. But certainly the great bulk
of you have professed to have put Him on. You have knelt
at this altar or some other altar and said: "I believe in Jesus
Christ as my Savior. That is the One who is my Master and
whose banner I intend to follow through life." But what are
you doing about it? How serious a matter is it for you?
Wake up! The putting on of Jesus is not something which is
to be taken lightly, but it is to be something which you regard
as the essential thing in life and without which you can
achieve nothing. No matter how successful you will be in
business, no matter how famous you may be, no matter how
often you may strive to find joy and happiness in life, it will
all fail you, leave you cold and dissatisfied, until you have
the satisfying, peace-giving love of God through Jesus Christ
to flood your soul and to put your heart at ease.

Recently a Jewish rabbi out East wrote a book which bears

the title *Peace of Mind*. Many people are buying that book.
Why do you suppose are they buying it? Because they are
looking for peace of mind. You can look for peace of mind
wherever you want. You will not find peace of mind until
God gives you the answer to the soul and to its needs. And
God has provided that answer in the sending of Jesus, your
Savior, your Redeemer. So don't be satisfied merely to know
that once you learned a few catechetical truths. Make it the
most serious part of your life, the steadfast concern of your
every thought, every prayer, to be in Christ, to learn how
to trust in Jesus, how to build the love of God in Christ into
everything in your life, and how to look at all of life through
the eyes of Jesus and His love so that you understand life
correctly, so that you can meet life face to face with courage
and the assurance of ultimate victory.

If we do have some among us this morning who never yet
have accepted Christ, I certainly want to plead with them
to do so. There is no other answer. There is no other way of
getting real peace of mind. The psychiatrist can help you talk
out the things that are inside of you. He can help you find
out where your troubles are and what out of the past is prey-
ing on you and distorting your life, but when he has accomplished all of that, he must send you to Christ to get the
answer, because it is only through Christ that you can get
rid of the sense of guilt, that your inner tensions can be
removed. No man in this world knows any other answer; so
don't look. Don't waste your time. Take the answer which
God gives you. Clothe yourself with Christ's holiness. He
shed His precious blood so that your sins should be washed
away. He is ready to take the garment of His righteousness
and put it around you and cover all your sins so that when
the Father looks down on you, He sees men and women just

as spotless as Jesus Himself. All the stains and scars are gone, and there is only purity because of Christ.

PUT OFF THE WORKS OF DARKNESS

When we trust in Jesus, then such trust must be followed by other things in life which are in harmony with it, and so Paul says: *"Put off the works of darkness."* Cast off the works of darkness. He tells us what some of these works of darkness are. He says: "Rioting and drunkenness, chambering and wantonness ['debauchery and lasciviousness' in more modern language], strife and envying [or, as the more recent Revised Standard Version has it, 'quarreling and jealousy']." These are the works of darkness. You and I have no difficulty in recognizing them, do we? They make up so much of our modern life. Rioting and drunkenness—the other evening, when we came out of a meeting at the Merchandise Mart, we encountered a fine young man, well built, apparently well endowed by his Creator with a good mind and appealing personality, but paralyzed with liquor. What a pitiful spectacle! We saw another man and a woman, probably his wife. He was so intoxicated, his wife could hardly hold him up. Is that something strange in the American scene? Go where you will, and you can find it in what are supposed to be the most exclusive night spots. There they are, men and women who are supposed to be refined and cultured, who probably would be very indignant if someone were to say that they were drunkards, living as God's children cannot live, as God will not have His children live. God will not allow the American people who want to swim in liquor to go on and on. God has given us many fine gifts, but He will not allow any of them to be misused. Why talk about that in a Christian Church? Need we fear that anybody in this church is going to be a sot or that we are going to live as the world lives? My friends, don't let us be simple! Let us at least be alert to the dangers in which we find ourselves.

How we respond to the things which go on in this world is so evident in our congregational life. When the national income of our country goes up 10 per cent, the income of the Church goes up about 10 per cent. When the income of the American people goes down, our income in the Church goes down just about in like measure. This shows us how responsive we are to the things that go on around us. We are in this world, and we are influenced and affected by the things that go on in this world. My heart goes out to you when I think how many of you are right out there day after day, face to face with the world and all of its temptations. When I think of that, then I say, this is the day when we want to issue the warning of Paul and say: "Wake up, wake up! Don't be asleep. Don't let yourself be destroyed before you realize what is really going on."

Debauchery and lasciviousness—Paul says these are the works of darkness. Are they? Well, read the newspapers. See what sisters say about sisters when they are having a divorce trial, what husbands say about wives and wives about husbands. Read the accounts of your daily newspaper, and see what people are doing. It is incredible. I don't think there was anything in Sodom or Gomorrah or in any of the peoples of the past that surpassed anything that is being done now in the way of debauchery and lasciviousness. There is not a person in this audience this morning who can say, "Oh, that would never happen to me." Wake up, my friend! Tomorrow it may be you. Maybe yet today if you don't wake up. Each of us is capable of every and any evil deed any other human being anywhere in this world is capable of. It is not for a single one of us to turn up his nose and to go through life as though he were immune. Wake up. Put on Jesus Christ and cast off the works of darkness.

PUT ON THE ARMOR OF LIGHT

Instead of doing as the world does, put on the armor of light. *"Let us put on the armor of light."* "Let us walk honestly as in the day." Let us not make "provision for the flesh to fulfill the lusts thereof," but let us walk as the children of God and in reverent regard of the holy will of our Creator. That is how we should live.

When we have put on Jesus and been covered with the cloak of righteousness, then we must look at Jesus and see how He lived. What did He do? How did He behave Himself in relationship to others? See how Jesus did; then you get a pattern to follow.

This text stands in immediate relationship to some things which Paul said about Christian love and Christian life, not quarreling, not jealousy, such as is in the world and such as can very easily come into the life of a Christian church or into a Christian home or any Christian institution, but love, so that in our response to the Savior, who has loved us, we try to express love in our relationship to God, to one another, to all our fellow men.

Now, of course, we could speak for hours on that subject by itself; but you take it and you apply it to your life wherever you find yourself, whether you are a son, a daughter, a father, a mother, an employer, an employee. Whatever your position in life may be, apply to it the law of love. If we will wake up, if we will put on Christ, if we will heed the warning of Christ and see that the night is far spent and that the day is at hand, then we will try to make the most of the opportunities we have now. And it is to this great adventure in Christian living, in the service of God, for the good of humanity—to this the Spirit of God would arouse us this morning, and to this I, as His humble spokesman, challenge and call you.

There Is Hope

❖ ❖ ❖

For whatsoever things were written aforetime were written for our learning, that we through patience and comfort of the Scriptures might have hope. Now, the God of patience and consolation grant you to be like-minded one toward another according to Christ Jesus, that ye may with one mind and one mouth glorify God, even the Father of our Lord Jesus Christ. Wherefore receive ye one another, as Christ also received us to the glory of God. Now I say that Jesus Christ was a minister of the circumcision for the truth of God to confirm the promises made unto the fathers, and that the Gentiles might glorify God for His mercy, as it is written: For this cause I will confess to Thee among the Gentiles and sing unto Thy name. And, again, He saith: Rejoice, ye Gentiles, with His people. And again: Praise the Lord, all ye Gentiles; and laud Him, all ye people. And, again, Esaias saith: There shall be a root of Jesse, and He that shall rise to reign over the Gentiles, in Him shall the Gentiles trust. Now, the God of hope fill you with all joy and peace in believing, that ye may abound in hope through the power of the Holy Ghost.

ROMANS 15:4-13.

"There is hope!" That, my friends, is the great and blessed truth which, by divine grace, I should like to write indelibly upon the heart of each of you on this Advent Sunday. "There is hope."

A great many people do not realize this fact. They have been disappointed so often in life, they have become so deceived and disillusioned on so many occasions that they have given up the idea that there is such a thing as a definite, sure, and certain hope.

HOPE NOT FOUND IN HUMAN ACHIEVEMENT

Many human beings placed their trust for a happy life and a beautiful world in the accomplishments of the scientists. The scientists failed. Instead of producing something that was beautiful, they produced an atomic bomb, which brought unheard-of terror to the hearts of men.

Many placed their reliance upon education. But the educators failed them, because some of the most-educated nations in the world became most war-minded.

Many placed their hope and trust in the economist, in the industrialist. They hoped that production would be the answer to mankind's troubles. But one day it happened that the smokestacks no longer belched forth smoke. The wheels of industry stopped turning. The world found itself in the grip of a universal depression, and all the wise men knew not what to do.

Many who are without hope today turn confidently to government. There are millions in a land like Italy or Germany or Russia who believed that the government would have the answer. If only they would let the government lead the way, then all would be well. Think how many have become pitifully disillusioned since that confidence first took root! Today we have many millions in all parts of the globe who are hopefully looking to the counsels of the United Nations, but with each passing day the hope that this organization will find the answer to humanity's difficulties and usher in a day of peace and joy and happiness grows more and more dim. So it is a fact, there are, as the Scriptures put it, a great many people who are "without God and without hope" in this world.

PERSONAL FEELING OF HOPELESSNESS

When we speak of people who are without hope, you and I know a little bit of what we are saying, because there are times when our hearts, too, seem to be devoid of hope. When life becomes so topsy-turvy, when our heartaches get to be so acute, and when the burdens that rest upon our shoulders come to be so heavy that we don't know where to turn any more, then sometimes it also looks to us as though there were nothing we had reason to hope for.

Maybe you are afflicted with some kind of an illness which doctors don't know how to handle; maybe you have someone who is very near and dear to you who has been crippled or afflicted in one way or another, and medical science can't do a thing about it, and it seems as though all of your prayers have gone unheard and unanswered; maybe you have some very, very heartbreaking situation in your home, against which you've been fighting and battling now for some time. It may under such circumstances look to you as though it were of no use trying to go on, as though there were nothing upon which you could really base a sound and solid hope. Perhaps some of you who are out there fighting the battles of life in the world of business and of industry find yourselves confronted with what seem to be insuperable problems and difficulties. Well, all of us, at one time or another, are inclined to be without hope. Doubt seizes our hearts and our minds and a dark cloud of gloom settles upon our spirits. It is as though there were nothing worth living for any more.

Just how tragic such a situation can be was brought to the attention of the whole world in a very dramatic manner when but a very short time ago one of the truly representative statesmen of America put a gun to his own head and ended his own life just after he had completed his account of his experiences in the Second World War.

In a world in which there are so many people without God and without hope, in a world in which you and I are tempted on occasion to yield our hearts and spirits to an attitude of cynical bitterness and hopelessness—in such a world and life I want to say to you this morning, "There is hope."

HOPE WELL FOUNDED

If this were nothing more than an assertion on my part, it would not have very great importance, because then it would only be an empty word. Or if it were merely the sentiment of a poet who expressed himself in a dramatic way, it wouldn't amount to very much. It would be a lovely sentiment, but it wouldn't have any real meaning. But that isn't the case. This statement which I am making is a statement of God which He rests on great historic facts.

When God says to you, "There is hope," He says it against the background of a great promise, which He fulfilled in a most wonderful way. When man first fell into sin and deprived himself of the blessedness of Paradise, God, his Creator, came to him with an encouraging, uplifting message of love. He told him that in due course He would send a Savior and that this Savior would again overcome the powers of evil and free him from the difficulties into which he had gotten himself. Years, decades, centuries passed by. God did not forget His promise. As a matter of fact, He reiterated it. At strategic periods of human history He again and again sent yet another voice to tell, in the language of the people of a given day and living under given circumstances, the story of this coming Messiah. Everybody who was familiar with the writings of the Old Testament was acquainted with this promise.

Beyond that, God did not only *tell* of a Messiah who was to come, but He gave a visual, living, impressive, dramatic demonstration of what was to happen. He gave to His people a very pronounced body of rituals and religious ceremonies. His people were not to observe these ceremonies merely as a matter of form. These colorful ceremonies were intended by God to keep His people ever mindful of the fact that a Messiah was going to come. This was what He had promised. This was what He wanted them to remember.

THE PROMISE FULFILLED

Paul, in the words of our text, now sets forth this beautiful fact: God kept His promise. If God had given promise to man and not kept His promise, then whereon would we build our hopes? On the ever-changing, shifting sands of time? on the uncertain circumstances of life as we find them? You couldn't build any hope on that sort of thing. And when the humans to whom you have looked fail you, then where would you go for hope? But now, says the Apostle Paul, no matter what may or may not have failed, God did not fail. God kept His promise. Jesus was sent in fulfillment of what God had promised to do.

My friends, that is the thing which makes Christianity so wonderful. Sometimes people have spun religious thoughts and ethical codes out of their own minds. They have succeeded in expressing their thoughts in most beautiful language. It all sounds so lovely and impressive, but when you begin to analyze it, you discover that it is nothing more than a matter of words. But it is different with the religion of the true God and of Jesus, whom He sent. Here you are dealing not only with words, but with an historic fact, with a Person who came into this world in fulfillment of the prophetic promises which God had given. So when I say to you this morning, "There is hope," I trust the Spirit of God will make very plain to you that this is not only a human assertion, but a divine truth which rests on the great historic fact that God kept His promise. And in the unfailing truthfulness of God lies our hope, because the Son of God did come. He did allow Himself to be born of a virgin. He did suffer and die as the atoning Sacrifice for the sins of all mankind.

HOPE FOR ALL

Our text not only assures us that there is hope, but it also sets forth in a most beautiful and impressive way, through quotations from the Old Testament, that this hope is intended for all people. The Children of Israel in Old Testament times, when well instructed, understood that. Theirs was always an aggressive, missionary religion. No properly instructed Israelite ever believed that only Israelites were to be the beneficiaries of the Messiah's great redemptive love and suffering. No, they knew that this Messiah would come for all, and our text sets this forth when it says: "And that the Gentiles might glorify God for His mercy, as it is written: For this cause I will confess to Thee among the Gentiles and sing unto Thy holy name. And, again, He saith: Rejoice, ye Gentiles, with His people."

So the hope whereof I am speaking this morning is not a hope limited to a handful of people, a hope intended by God only for members of a certain race or for the people living in a certain day or a given country. This is a universal hope.

It is a hope which is offered to every man born of woman. There is no person so high or so low, so white or so black, so literate or so illiterate, but God's hope is offered to that person. It makes no difference whatsoever who you are, God wants to say to you this morning: "There is hope for you. God loves you. Jesus has taken your sins away."

BLESSED FRUITS
PEACE

And out of this beautiful and blessed fact shall come the things whereof our text speaks; first of all, the gift of peace. "Now, the God of hope," says Paul, "fill you with all joy and *peace* in believing." Peace—we talk of world peace, and it is proper that we should, but what we often forget is the fact that we cannot have world peace unless the people who make up this human family have peace in their own hearts. As long as the hearts of men are filled with fear, with bitterness and with hatred; as long as people don't know how to spend a quiet moment resting in God, so long you cannot have a world of peace. Individuals who are being haunted and tormented by terrors of one kind or another by day and by night can neither have peace in their own hearts nor live at peace with their fellow men. But when you accept the Christ, when you put your faith in Him as the One whom God sent in fulfillment of His Messianic promises to save your soul from sin and death, then you find peace. No matter how disturbed life may then be on the outside, you will have found a secret, the secret of God's children. You will know how quietly to put your trust in the loving God. Howsoever the storms may blow, you will know that you are securely sheltered in His protecting embrace. Peace—God sent Jesus, that is why you and I can have peace within. Many circumstances and experiences may tend to disturb us, but nothing can ever get so far down in our hearts as to rob us of that inner, profound, heavenly peace.

And where there is that peace, there, as Paul puts it, will also be joy. It is true, if you and I undertook to look at all the negative sides of life, we could make this appear to be a very ugly world in which there is absolutely no good. But that isn't the only side there is to life. That isn't the only thing God wants you and me to look at. God has put a lot of good and beautiful things into this world. As His children you and I should be conscious of those good things. We have our own homes. We have dear ones who love us. We can gather with them in the living room of an evening or sit with them around the dinner table. We can exchange kindnesses. We can be thoughtful and considerate of one another. We can make life so sweet and decent for one another that we have abundant reason to thank God for the joy that He has given to us. We have our tasks to perform. If we want to think only of the fact that we must work and that some of our work is unpleasant, life may become very bitter and forbidding. But if we will think that each day this God who has redeemed us and who loves us gives us strength so that we can work, gives us human beings whom we can serve through our skills and our knowledge and learning of whatever type it may be, then, you see, life becomes beautiful. When you look out and realize that the sun again sends forth his life-giving, warming rays, that the trees and the mountains, the rivers and the lakes, all retain their majesty year after year; when we remember that God has given us a world in which birds can sing to delight our souls, see, then we

can have joy. When you think of the things that men do in
their revolt against God, of the sins and iniquities whereof
they make themselves guilty, then life is ugly indeed; but
if you think of what God, who has fulfilled His promise, does
for you and what He has given to this world, then joy may
well fill your soul.

HOPE

And beyond all this, says Paul, there comes this hope.
There is hope. He says: "The God of hope fill you with all
joy and hope in believing, that ye may abound in hope
through the power of the Holy Ghost." Life is a terrible
thing if you think of yourself as a clock that is running down.
Then you haven't very much farther to go. Then the day
will come very, very quickly when it will be all over. But if
you believe that Jesus died for you and rose again; if you
believe that even as God kept His promise and sent the
Messiah, so the Messiah will keep His promises in which He
says: "Where I am, there shall also My servant be," "Because
I live, ye shall live also," then you know that you are not a
clock which is running down. You are rather a traveler who
is making a journey. You have your eye on the goal. From
eternity shines the light of hope which brightens the whole
pathway of human existence. Here, there, on this side, on
that, you may observe and experience unpleasantnesses of one
kind or another, but never do you take your eye off that
goal. You do not go downward, but you go steadily upward.
You know that with each tick of the clock, with each heart-
beat, you are coming closer and closer to the realization of
your ultimate hope. One day you are going to be with God.
You see: "There is hope." Life's story is not all told in the
experiences of our few earthly years. Life's story extends into

eternity, and we who come from God are to go back to God.

Yes, there is hope, and because there is hope, you and I are under such great obligation to the God of hope. He has not allowed us to be as empty as we should be had He left us to our own doing. We by our sins almost try desperately to make life empty, hollow, sordid, meaningless. But God comes to us in His love. He strives to overcome this emptiness and by His love to give meaning and fullness to our existence. He keeps the light of hope burning within.

Because He does that, you and I are under such a great debt of love to God. This debt of love we should discharge. We should express our gratitude and our appreciation. Paul tells us how. If there is hope in your heart, if you are thrilled with the fact that God kept His promise and sent His Savior to redeem you, then show it. He says: "Now, the God of patience and consolation grant you to be like-minded one toward another according to Christ Jesus, that ye may with one mind and one mouth glorify God, even the Father of our Lord Jesus Christ. Wherefore receive ye one another, as Christ also received us to the glory of God."

God asks one thing. If we appreciate the fact that He has given us a foundation upon which to build a safe and certain hope, and that He has ignited fires of love within our hearts, then we should thank Him by living a life of love. We should have love toward one another. There should be in us the kind of mind that was in Christ. Christ came not to be ministered unto, but to minister. He came not to be sought out, but to seek. He came because He loved us. And it is such love we should have in our hearts for one another.

I think you all realize how far we fall short in this particular. We don't need to make many words about our deficiencies in this respect. We manifest our selfishness and love-lessness in countless ways. You can think so quickly how that is done in your own home, how thoughtless you often are, how by your selfishness you introduce a note of strife and discord into your own family life.

We observe it here in the church. There are some folks in the church who would never turn a hand to do anything for the church. Let somebody else do it. There are some folks who may be richly blessed by God and who have very sub-stantial incomes but who make no effort to share proportion-ately with the church. They are perfectly willing that some-body else who may not be nearly so well situated should bear a disproportionate part of the responsibility. And so this lovelessness runs right through life. Well, my friends, if human society is to become more beautiful, if there are to be happier relationships among men, that start must be made among the Christians, among the people who know there is hope; who live like people who have hope; who thrill to the fact that they possess a hope; who show their appreciation by the life of love which they live.

May the Spirit of God kindle within the heart of each one of us the light of hope, and may He give us the power to let that light shine forth by a life of love.

How to Be Strong, Decisive, Victorious

❖ ❖ ❖

Let a man so account of us as of the ministers of Christ and stewards of the mysteries of God. Moreover, it is required in stewards that a man be found faithful. But with me it is a very small thing that I should be judged of you or of man's judgment; yea, I judge not mine own self. For I know nothing by myself, yet am I not hereby justified; but He that judgeth me is the Lord. Therefore judge nothing before the time, until the Lord come, who both will bring to light the hidden things of darkness and will make manifest the counsels of the hearts. And then shall every man have praise of God.—I CORINTHIANS *4:1-5.*

A young mother was speaking to me about a sick child. She said that earlier in the life of the child she and her husband had been given certain medical advice with reference to his care. Now she was considerably troubled, wondering whether it might not have been better had they done something else. Is there anybody in this house of worship this morning, male or female, young or old, who does not know what was going on in that mother's heart? This is one of the problems we all have in life. We find it so difficult to live strongly, confidently, and to act decisively. We are inclined to review the things that we have done, to question our judgments, and to worry. We say to ourselves: "I wonder whether it would not have been better had I done that." Few things in life go to weaken us more than does such want of decision. If you spend your life wondering and worrying whether you hadn't done better to have done this or to have done that, you are not going to have a strong, happy, confident, victorious life.

BE FAITHFUL

Well, how shall we get strength for such a life? *Where and how may we learn to live confidently and decisively?* Thank God, Paul gives us the answer in the words of the Epistle for today, which was read to you from the lectern. *The first principle Paul lays down for confident, assured, strong, decisive living is this: "Be found faithful."*

Be faithful, wherever you are, whatever you are. Each of you occupies some place in life. The one is a husband, a father, the other a wife, a mother, a son, a daughter, a brother, a sister, an employer, a workman, a professional man, and so on. Each of you is occupying some place in life. Each of you has been given certain qualities, certain endowments. The physical vigor and health of the one may be very much better than that of the other. One may be able to think more rapidly, more profoundly, than another. One may have much greater powers of endurance, of concentration, of application, than another. One may have enjoyed vastly finer privileges of training and broader experiences in life than the other. God is not expecting *you* to do what somebody else may be able to do. God is expecting that you should do in your place what you are able to do with the opportunities, the qualities, the abilities, which He has given to you.

Paul had to face this very clearly. He wrote the words of

this Epistle in answer to a situation which obtained in the
Christian church at Corinth. The Corinthian Christians were
sadly divided into factions. Some of them said, "We are the
followers of Apollos." Apollos was a very polished gentleman
who possessed the gift of oratory in an exceptional degree.
Some of these people were fascinated by Apollos and his
preaching. They said, "That is the kind of a minister we
want." Others did not think so much of Apollos. They were
much more impressed with Peter. They said: "Peter comes
from the mother church at Jerusalem. He is the one who has
the authoritative message. That is the one we are going to
follow." Others said: "We are not impressed with Apollos
and his oratory, we are not impressed with Peter and the
background of his Jerusalem experiences; we believe in Paul.
That is our man. He is a man of courage and a man of vision.
He is the man, after all, who came and brought us the Gospel.
That is the man we are going to follow." So they were sadly
divided, each making his choice.

What was Paul to do in the situation? He had to try to
teach these people that they had no right to expect Apollos
to be like himself, and they had no right to expect him to be
like Peter. The only thing they had a right to expect was
that all of them be found faithful.

DO YOUR BEST

This does not apply only to Christian ministers and
teachers. This applies to every person in every walk of life.
Not all wives are going to be equally good housekeepers,
equally good cooks, equally wise in the understanding of
child psychology. Not all businessmen are going to be able
to operate on the same large and successful scale. Not every
professional man is going to be equally brilliant in the pursuit
of his particular endeavors in life. God does not expect it,

and man has no right to expect it, and you should not let your heart be made heavy because somebody else can do a thing better than you can do it. That is not what you are to be judged by. Nor is any of you to judge himself by it. The thing that matters is: Are you faithful in your place? Not all the young men and women who study at Concordia will secure A's. There will be those who will get their B's and C's and D's. But that is not the important thing. The important thing is that every student do the best he or she can with such health and such talents as God has given to him.

God does not expect all preachers to preach with the same eloquence and the same power. All that He expects is that every pastor do the best that he can in his place with what God has given to him. If I call on someone who is a prospective member of the church, my approach may be of one kind. If another pastor calls, his approach may be of an entirely different kind. He is not asking me to do my work as the other pastor does his, nor is He asking the other pastor to do his work as I do mine. The only thing He is asking is that we both be found faithful. And this applies to you wherever you are.

JESUS WAS FAITHFUL

The glory of Christianity is that Jesus was faithful. Jesus came into this world to do a specific task. He was very lowly, very humble, but He did the one thing for which He came. He redeemed you. That is why it is possible for me to tell you over and over the beautiful story of God's redeeming love in Christ. It doesn't make any difference who you are, Jesus came for you. It matters not what sins have stained your soul, Jesus has paid for those sins. It matters not how great your guilt and iniquity, the Lord has atoned for all of it. He gave Himself on Calvary's Cross in fulfillment of His duty and for the completion of your salvation. This is to bring sweet comfort to you. It is to make you realize that with a heart free from sin and guilt you can boldly look up to your heavenly Father as to One who loves you and who puts His arms of mercy and grace about you.

This work which Jesus did should not only provide you with the comfort of forgiveness and with the blessed hope of eternal salvation, but it should also be within you the one driving force which causes you to try, and to try again, to apply yourself faithfully to your duties in life. Paul said: "Let a man so account of us as of the ministers of Christ and stewards of the mysteries of God. Moreover, it is required in stewards that a man be found faithful." As the Christian minister has the responsibility faithfully to teach the Word of God, faithfully to minister unto immortal souls, so every Christian has the responsibility in his particular place in life to live out the fulfillment of his duties as faithfully as he or she can. That is basic in the living of a strong, confident, decisive life.

IN THE LIGHT OF ETERNITY

"But," you say, "that is not all there is to life. If it were only up to me to deal with this situation, I think I could manage it all right. But I live in a world of human beings, and so I am always being influenced by the opinions and attitudes of others." Paul knew all about that; so, to meet this situation, he said to the Christians at Corinth: "Those are not the great considerations. *The thing for you to do is to live your life in the light of eternity.*" The old Church Fathers perhaps would have said, *sub specie aeternitatis,* against the backdrop of eternity. Listen to Paul: "With me it is a very small thing that I should be judged of you or of man's judgment; yea, I judge not mine own self. For I know nothing by myself, yet am I not hereby justified; but He that judgeth me is the Lord. Therefore judge nothing before the time, until the Lord come, who both will bring to light the hidden things of darkness and will make manifest the counsels of the hearts. And then shall every man have praise of God."

Paul knew what it meant to have people disapprove of the things he did. When he preached the Law, the Gentiles said: "That is too severe. You can't expect us to live by such a Law." When he preached the Gospel to the Jews, they said: "That is too easy." Paul knew what it meant to be criticized, to have people question his motives, to wonder whether he was altogether sincere and honest about what he was doing. So this was the way in which he faced that situation. And this is the only way in which you and I ever will be able to face it.

You know how you feel about public criticism. You don't like it! How many times in your life have you already failed to do what in your heart you felt you ought to do because you did not want to be criticized for it? I am sure that many fine things in life are left undone because people fear criticism, the disapproval of their family or of their fellow men. Many a businessman might be willing to sit down and work out a totally different program for his business in relationship to his employees if he didn't fear that the whole trade would bear down on him if he did so. Many a workingman would say: "This is unfair. I don't think these demands which are being made upon my boss at the present time are right and just. I am going to work. I am satisfied with my working conditions." Many a man would say that—if he were not afraid of the criticism which would come to him. It is unbelievable how many things are left undone, or how many things are done, not because of the conviction of the individual heart and conscience, but only because people are afraid of being judged. I have known of instances in which wives were

ashamed to have more babies because they were afraid they
would be criticized for the size of their family. I am sure
there are men and women in this very community who would
be members of this church if they were not afraid of criticism.
I have had occasion to say to big, strong, broad-shouldered
men: "There is only one reason why you don't come into the
Kingdom of God, and that is because you are a coward. You
are afraid of what people will say." Such a power public
opinion and the attitude of our fellow men have in determin-
ing our own conduct.

Paul says, "You can't live a strong life that way. Why, I
cannot even be guided by my judgment of myself. I know
nothing of myself." He felt he was doing the best he knew
how, but that was no assurance. How could he be certain
that his own judgment was perfect? How could he be sure
that he was not having some motives within him which were
so subtle that he was not personally aware of them? Hence
Paul did not feel able to evaluate the wisdom and the right-
ness of all that he had done. "No," he said, "the fact that I
do not know anything bad in what I am doing does not mean
that I am perfect. I do not even judge myself. And what is
more, I am not even concerned about your judgment." "With
me it is a very small thing that I should be judged of you or
of man's judgment. Yea, I judge not mine own self." Paul
knew, on the one hand, you could not let the public deter-
mine for you what you should do or should not do, and, on
the other hand, you could not do something just because the
public approved of it.

UNSAFE GUIDE

In the moral life of the world today and particularly in
these United States of America more and more individuals
who are analyzing present-day American behavior are be-

coming aware of this particular truth. We have, on the one hand, a great cry for personal freedom. Everybody stands on his rights. Everybody wants to do just what he wants to do, and he doesn't want anybody to interfere with him. On the other hand, so few people are willing to assume personal responsibility for what they do. They do what they do because it has mass approval. Many say: "That is what everybody is doing. Why, that is how everybody thinks about it. The public doesn't seem to think this is so wrong. And because the public doesn't think it is so wrong, therefore it cannot be so wrong."—Oh, no, you cannot accept any moral guidance of such a nature. You cannot let the public tell you what to do, nor can you let the public tell you what not to do, because if you do, you will never know where you are. You will never have the solid foundations of moral and spiritual certainty under your feet.

Just think where you will be if you let public opinion tell you something about churchgoing. What is the prevailing attitude on that matter? First of all, a great many people don't care enough to think about it, and many others frankly don't believe in going. Their pet answer is: "Why go to church? I would rather stay home and be sincere than go to church and be a hypocrite." How easy and superficial such an attitude is!

How can you let the American public decide for you such moral questions as sobriety and moderation? The American conscience is no longer very sensitive on the question of excessive drinking. It has almost taken for granted that some of the very people who occupy some of the most prominent positions in American society will yield to the excessive use of alcoholic liquor. Well, if we have nothing to be concerned about except public attitude, then it doesn't make any difference whether we are drunkards or not. But the question is

not at all: What does the mass of people think, or what will
the public stand for or not stand for? Well, then, how shall
we decide this? Paul says: "There is only one sure way in
which you can do it. That is in the light of eternity." Against
the backdrop of this great outstanding truth of Advent, *the
Lord is coming again to judge the world in righteousness.*
It is only when you look at your life in the light of this truth
that you can be sure and strong and confident.

He says: "Therefore judge nothing before the time, until
the Lord come, who both will bring to light the hidden
things of darkness and will make manifest the counsels of the
heart." This is a part of the great message of Advent: Jesus
is coming again. The Bible has so much to say about it, and
we do so little with it. The other day I was reading an article,
as I told the adults in our lecture group this morning, on the
preachers and the atomic bomb. This writer was a bit impatient with certain kinds of preachers. He said: "Some of
these preachers in the past refused to talk about the return-
ing Christ, Judgment, heaven, and hell. They ridiculed the
idea of hell-fire. But now these same preachers are standing
before their audiences trying to give them a scientific lecture
on the atomic bomb and trying to beat them into religion by
holding the threat of this bomb over them." It is not the
things that you and I may conjure up, however significant
they may be, that matter; it is the great fact that Jesus is
coming again to judge the world in righteousness which
matters.

GOD JUDGES

You and I are to live our lives faithfully in the full assurance that whether they are right or whether they are wrong
is not going to be decided by our personal judgment, our
own ideas or rationalizations, or by the judgments and ap-

provals or disapprovals of our contemporaries in human society, but by the Lord. You and I will be judged by the Word. "The Word that I have spoken, the same shall judge him in the Last Day." At that time human hearts will be laid open. Then will be determined what the motives of people are. You and I are not to sit pointing the finger at each other, questioning each other's motives, honesty, sincerity of purpose and of faith. No, that is a matter for Him who is going to expose our innermost sentiments to inspection and full view. We are to be faithful.

God has given us His holy Word. He has told us who our Savior is. He has laid out for us the way in which we are to walk. It is for us to accept this Savior, to walk in that way of godliness and righteousness as the Spirit of God gives us strength and ability. In this we are to be a help to one another. In this we are to be sympathetic toward one another in our common weaknesses and failures. And then we are to carry on and await the Great Day when Jesus comes, "who both will bring to light the hidden things of darkness and will make manifest the counsels of the hearts."

So don't waste your life worrying about what the people will say, what the people will think. You cannot live a strong life by any such principles. Don't waste your time, your energies, and don't weaken yourself and so confuse and perplex yourself that you are incapable of strong living, by worrying about the things in the past and saying: "I wonder whether I shouldn't have done this or that." No, be faithful. Commit your life into the hands and the keeping of Almighty God, and let Him be the Judge. If you faithfully cling to this Christ and steadfastly seek to serve Him where you are in life as best you can, then He one day will let all know that yours was a heart of love, of faithful devotion to Him. And no matter how smooth and clever the deceiver and the hypocrite may be, no matter how successful he may appear to be by way of doing violence to the will and ways of God and cruelly abusing his fellow men, not one shall escape. Not one shall pass the all-seeing eye of Him who will come to judge.

I hope the Spirit of God will help each of us to see these great truths clearly, so that against the backdrop of eternity we may each faithfully apply ourselves to each given task. Then we can wait with joy for the coming of the Christ.

How to Be Happy

❖   ❖   ❖

*Rejoice in the Lord alway; and again I say, Rejoice. Let your moderation be known unto all men. The Lord is at hand. Be careful for nothing; but in everything by prayer and supplication, with thanksgiving, let your requests be made known unto God. And the peace of God, which passeth all understanding, shall keep your hearts and minds through Christ Jesus.—*PHILIPPIANS *4:4-7.*

Paul, the Apostle, speaks to us in the Epistle of today about a subject in which we are all interested. He speaks of happiness. You would like to be happy. I should like to be happy. All men would like to be happy. What is more, our Creator wants us to be happy. If you had asked Paul, "Which is the surest, shortest, straightest road to happiness?" he would have said, "Be a Christian." Paul's answer would have sounded, and to this day still does sound, altogether incredible to a great many people.

MISCONCEPTIONS

Many folks, as you know without my telling you, have the idea that Christianity does more to kill joy in human life than any other one thing in this world. Men have conceived of the Ten Commandments and the moral requirements of the Christian religion as an insufferable interference with a good time and real happiness. So the world has decided to turn its back on Christianity and to seek happiness in its own way. Men have felt that if you really wanted to be happy, you must seek your happiness in this world's goods. I don't know how many Americans this morning have the idea that happiness lies in material things, but I am sure the number is large. Proportionately we should probably find the same thing to be true in other lands as well.

Because men have thought that material possessions would make for happiness, nations have gone out and fought wars trying to increase their holdings. Instead of finding happiness, they found death, bloodshed, destruction, woes and miseries that sometimes endured for generations. Great captains of industry and commerce in our country who thought that real happiness was to be found in material possessions pursued their own ideas, but they did not find happiness. They brought upon themselves and the American people strife and conflict between the employer and the employee. They are the creators of the racketeer in the American labor unions of today. Their greed and avarice caused blood to be shed, government to interfere in ever greater measure in the life of the American people and in the management of business affairs. They did not find happiness. So man, forsaking the ways of God and pursuing his own ideas in the matter, has brought misery and woe upon himself.

Others have not been so much concerned about money and material possessions. They have sought for happiness in the satisfaction of carnal lusts. Again man has failed to find the thing he looked for. This kind of living has produced broken homes, masses of unhappy children, diseased bodies and minds, a chapter of misery and tragedy which no words of human tongue could describe in too lurid a fashion.

Man going his own way and refusing to heed God's way has not found happiness. Men have sought for happiness in the satisfaction of personal pride, the pride of reason and the like, but again it has not been a road to happiness. While turning against God, revolting against divine authority, refusing to submit to the voice and the teachings of God, man has robbed himself of all peace and of all sound basis for true joy and true happiness. Think of the despair in human souls because they have nothing to rely upon except what their own limited little minds could suggest. If today we face a Christmas in which there are going to be many unhappy people, a Christmas in which many hearts are going to be very, very heavy, then this want of happiness, this stark tragedy in human life, is not due to God, but rather to man's refusal to listen to God. All our misery, all our want, all our suffering, we might say, is in direct proportion to the degree to which we stubbornly adhere to our way and reject God's way. Now, in the face of all this, Paul would like to give to you and to me the answer to our very important question, "What will make us happy people?"

BE CHRISTIANS

Paul says, "Be Christians. Rejoice in the Lord alway, and again I say, Rejoice." There is no doubt in Paul's mind as to what the attitude of the Christian heart should be and what kind of spirit should flood his soul. But there is also no doubt in his mind as to the way in which this can be accomplished. "Rejoice in the Lord alway." Well, what does that mean? How can we rejoice in the Lord? Paul tells us.

FIND PEACE WITH GOD

First, he would say, find "the peace of God which passeth

all understanding." This "shall keep your hearts and minds through Christ Jesus." It does not make very much difference how much money you have, nor how famous you are—if your soul is haunted, you cannot be happy. It is altogether useless talking about happiness unless you are at peace with God. So the very first step in the direction of happiness is to find peace with God. It was for the purpose of bringing this peace that Jesus came. That was why Isaiah could say 750 years before Christ's birth: "Unto us a Child is born, unto us a Son is given . . . and His name shall be called . . . the Prince of Peace." That is why the angels so jubilantly sang: "Glory to God in the highest, and on earth peace, good will toward men."

If you want happiness, take it. Look for it where God will have you find it. Come to Him in all humility of soul, and accept Jesus as your Redeemer. We have not a single person in this house of worship this morning whose soul and conscience have not been disturbed by a sense of personal guilt. There is nothing which robs you so quickly and so completely of all inner happiness as does the sense of guilt. God doesn't want you to go through life beaten down by a feeling of guilt and uncleanness. He wants you to be lifted up. He wants your face to glow with a divine radiance, as it were. There should shine from your eyes the light of joy and peace and happiness, because you know that Jesus came for you. He took away your sins. When you believe in Him as your personal Redeemer, then you have found peace with God. If you know as each day dawns, if you know as each day closes, that the eyes of a benevolent and loving God are looking down upon you, that all your sins and transgressions have been wiped out, then you can be quiet, then you can have peace and joy within you. I hope the Spirit of God will help each of you understand this truth so that you will take this first step toward happiness.

If you have taken it, then try to learn more fully just what it means. Feast your soul on that fact more completely. Suck out every drop of sweetness there is in it, because this is the real way to happiness.

TRUST IN GOD

Paul would say next: When you have found this peace, then put your trust in this God. That is the next step on the road to happiness. God does not only want to assure you of your forgiveness, He wants to help you in all other problems of life. Out of sin come many other difficulties and problems. God has an interest in all of them. He doesn't only want to relieve your mind from a sense of guilt. He wants to relieve your mind from every burden. This doesn't mean that you should not think any more, but it does mean that you should not worry any more. See, this is what Paul says: "Be careful for nothing," or, to put it in our kind of language, "Be full of care about nothing." Don't worry, or as the Revised Standard Version has it: "Have no anxiety."

There are many things in life because of which you have anxieties, worries. Sometimes it is your health or the health of some dear one. Sometimes it is your business. Sometimes it is your own moral and spiritual self. You feel yourself weak and slipping and failing here and there. Sometimes it is the general conditions in the world. Oh, there are so many things because of which we worry: home and family situations, concern about our children, their education, their development, their growth and maturity, and so on. There are literally a million things because of which we can be very much worried. These things can rest like a huge boulder on our hearts and weigh us down. They can make us feel as

Old Truths for a New Day

though there were nothing in life worth living for any more. You have had days like that, and so have I, but we are not to go through life that way. That is not how God wants us to feel. You are not happy when you feel as though you were being crushed by a huge load of worries and cares, and so the Apostle says: " 'Be careful for nothing.' Throw all your cares off. Put them on the Lord." He says: "Cast all your cares upon Him, for He careth for you." This means that you must trust God. Just as you must believe in Jesus to get the benefit of His redeeming love, just so you must trust a loving God to get the benefit of His help. How can God relieve you from the burdens of life if you insist upon carrying them all by yourself? No, let God carry them. He wants to carry them. He wants you to trust in Him for that.

PRAY

This trust should express itself. So Paul says: "The third thing you should do if you really want to be happy is pray. 'Be careful for [full of care about] nothing, but in everything by prayer and supplication, with thanksgiving, let your requests be made known unto God.' " Because we trust in God, we should come to God with all our heartaches, with all our needs. There is not a thing in this world that you can stand in need of about which God would not have you speak to Him in prayer. He has said: "Ask, and it shall be given you." "Whatsoever ye shall ask the Father in My name, He will give it you." If there is a real need in your life, if there is something that will actually contribute to your joy, your happiness, your temporal and your eternal well-being, talk to God about it, but have no doubt. Leave yourself entirely in His hands. Even as Jesus in the Garden of Gethsemane committed Himself into the Father's care, so you and I should with all that we are, with all that we have, with all that we hope to be, commit ourselves into the loving care of the heavenly Father.

In connection with this matter of prayer, Paul adds a little point which is most important. He says: "In everything by prayer and supplication, *with thanksgiving*, let your requests be made known unto God." Do you realize that one of the reasons why you and I often are so unhappy is that we do not count our blessings? You can give a man a beautiful home, situated on a lovely hill overlooking an enchanting and charmingly beautiful lake, and say to him: "This is yours; move in, enjoy it," only to have him hang his head and say: "What, only one, not two such homes? Where will I go in the winter, or where will I go in the summer? Why isn't this home like that home over there?" That is what you and I are doing to God all the time. God gives and gives and gives, but we insist upon thinking on those things which we do not have. Do you think there is anybody in this audience who could for one moment still hang his head and act disgruntled if he actually took time to count the blessings which God gives him? Is there anybody here who could make a long face and frown if he thought of all of God's goodness to him? No, the reason why we are such dissatisfied people, why we are always fighting and looking for something else, still is that we do not stop and count our blessings. So when you are asking God for the things that you need, you should at the same time also thank God for the things that He has given you and steadily is giving you. That is the way to happiness. If you do not appreciate what God gives you, it doesn't make the least difference how much He gives you, you will not be happy anyhow. So with our prayers that God might fill our needs should go our expressions of praise and

thanksgiving, that we might really respond with joy to the
fullness of God's goodness in our lives.

Finally, Paul has one other bit of advice for us who would
follow the road to happiness. This has to do with our attitude toward one another, toward all our fellow men. He says:
"Let your moderation be known unto all men. The Lord is at
hand." The word *moderation* is translated in various ways.
When you read it this way, you may think that it means
moderation in eating and drinking and the like. I think the
Revised Standard Version, which reads "forbearance," or the
translation "sweet reasonableness" come closer to the actual
meaning of what the Apostle meant to say: "Let your forbearance ['your sweet reasonableness'] be known unto all men."
If you want to be happy and find peace with God, trust God
for everything that you need in life, plead with God for those
things that are still wanting, and thank Him for those things
which He has given you, and then live in a spirit of forbearance and sweet reasonableness with your fellow men.

If you were to stop to think how much of your own personal happiness has been ruined because you have allowed
yourself to become all agitated by some faults and by some
weaknesses which you have observed in another person, I
think you would be quite surprised. So much of our happiness is ruined in just that way. It is not difficult for you to see
faults in me. Now, if you will let these faults get you down,
if you are going to make them a constant object of your
interest and your attention, you are not going to get any
pleasure out of my service to you. I will increasingly become
a source of irritation to you. In like manner I do not have
to be particularly wise to discover faults in you. If I were
to think every working day about all of the faults and all of

the weaknesses in the people who make up Grace Church, it would become utterly impossible to go on being the pastor of the church. One would become so irritated with you that one could no longer serve you with joy and satisfaction. There is only one way that you and I can get along, and that is by the spirit of forbearance. You must be forbearing in your attitude toward me, and I must be forbearing in my attitude toward you. We must have about us the spirit of Jesus Christ, the spirit of love, of kindness, of forgiveness. Only so can we be happy.

You have never yet in this world found a person happy that carried a feeling of bitterness in his heart, who was set against his fellow men, who was always looking for their faults. That sort of bitterness is the shortest road to misery and unhappiness. So in this Advent season, this happy season of expectation, Paul adds his final bit of counsel: Be forbearing in your attitude toward your fellow men. Let your general spirit of kindness and good will and sweet reasonableness be known to all. Only so can the light of joy be burning within you. Only so can your heart be kept from growing cold. Only so can you have a warm spirit that makes you feel good and that lets other people realize that you are indeed a son, a daughter, of God following Jesus.

THE LORD IS AT HAND

Paul reinforces his admonition with the reminder "The Lord is at hand." When you and I look about upon our fellow men, we should not sit in judgment on them and severely condemn them. We should rather let our hearts go out to them. Think of it, every day we come closer and closer to that great moment when the Lord is going to appear to judge the world in righteousness! What men need is pity, understanding, helpful living—not bitterness, not con-

demnation, not a holier-than-thou attitude, which looks down
on them, but one of kindly helpfulness and of Christian forgiving. Christmas is at hand. God has sent us the wonderful
Gift. He wants fullness of joy to be in the heart of each of us.
I hope the Spirit of God will make you, each one of you, wise
so that you will not pursue your own way, which leads to
misery and destruction, but accept God's way. Then you will
understand how it was possible for a man who was in prison,
for a man who was waiting for the executioner to come and
cut off his head, to write his letter of joy and to say to the
whole Christian world: "Rejoice in the Lord alway, and
again I say, Rejoice."

❖ ❖ ❖

God's Greatest Gift to Man

And it came to pass in those days that there went out a decree from Caesar Augustus that all the world should be taxed. (And this taxing was first made when Cyrenius was governor of Syria.) And all went to be taxed, everyone into his own city. And Joseph also went up from Galilee, out of the city of Nazareth, into Judea, unto the city of David, which is called Bethlehem (because he was of the house and lineage of David), to be taxed with Mary, his espoused wife, being great with child. And so it was that while they were there, the days were accomplished that she should be delivered. And she brought forth her first-born Son and wrapped Him in swaddling clothes and laid Him in a manger, because there was no room for them in the inn. And there were in the same country shepherds abiding in the field, keeping watch over their flock by night. And, lo, the angel of the Lord came upon them, and the glory of the Lord shone round about them, and they were sore afraid. And the angel said unto them: Fear not; for, behold, I bring you good tidings of great joy, which shall be to all people. For unto you is born this day in the city of David a Savior, which is Christ the Lord. And this shall be a sign unto you: Ye shall find the Babe wrapped in swaddling clothes, lying in a manger. And suddenly there was with the angel a multitude of the heavenly host praising God and saying: Glory to God in the highest, and on earth peace, good will toward men.—LUKE 2:1-14.

May it please God in His mercy, for Jesus' sake, to pour out His Holy Spirit upon each of us in rich measure so that we may all experience in our hearts the wonderful joys of this great and blessed day. Amen.

CHRISTMAS JOYS INCREASE

President Truman said in his address to the nation yesterday that Christmas was essentially a family festival. This is true in more ways than one. God in His surpassing love has made it possible for even little children to enjoy the spiritual significance of Christmas. If you were here last evening and saw that wonderful group of boys and girls, their shining eyes and their radiant countenances, telling the story of Christ and singing the beautiful Christmas carols, then you know that children can understand something of the beauty and the meaning of this holy day and of God's precious Gift to men. Christmas, however, is not only a children's festival, as some people erroneously suppose. The truth is that each succeeding Christmas in our lives should become more wonderful, more meaningful, more joyful, than any Christmas that has ever gone before. If your spiritual understanding is growing as your experiences in life multiply, the Gift of God at Christmastime should mean more to you this Christmas Day than it has ever before meant to you in all the years that have gone before. This is a great day of joy and filled with so much meaning because it is the day on which we commemorate God's greatest Gift to man.

JESUS THE SON OF GOD

God gives us many gifts: the air we breathe; the water we drink; the food we eat; the clothing we wear; the shelter which protects us. God gives us so many gifts that we could not in any amount of time present a complete catalog of them. But when God gives all other gifts, He takes of that which is His and gives it to us. When Christmas came, however, God took of Himself, as it were. That was what the angel said: "Unto you is born this day in the city of David a Savior, which is *Christ the Lord.*" Here God, the eternal One, the Son of God, becomes man. Even God can give us no greater gift than Himself.

It is because of the very greatness and uniqueness of this Gift that Christians have responded to it and that even unbelieving children of the world have been impressed. This is the season when everybody gives gifts. People who otherwise throughout the year may be penurious, stingy, and tight-fisted will loosen up at Christmas time and give something to somebody, because there is something of the irresistible about God's great Gift to man. Every gift which you gave this Christmas, and every gift which you have received, is only a symbol and a reminder of this great Gift. Nothing in the history of the world has so touched human hearts as did this Gift. This has unloosed a flood of gifts and an expression of good will such as no other event and no other character in history has even remotely occasioned.

Sometimes people talk as though Jesus were only one of a great galaxy of outstanding religious and humanitarian leaders. They will mention Buddha, Confucius, Mohammed, Florence Nightingale, Abraham Lincoln, and a variety of others. In that number they will include Jesus, as though He were only one of many. My friends, let me ask you: Do you know of anyone who has so touched the human heart as Jesus did? Why, even the coldest and most mercenary materialist, who is interested only in the improved business which grows out of the purchase of Christmas gifts, must admit that he doesn't know anyone who has so influenced the hearts of men and called forth such an outpouring of gifts and good will as has Jesus.

JESUS, OUR SAVIOR

There is a reason for that. Jesus was not only a great man. He not only lived a good life, but Jesus is our Savior. That was what the heavenly ambassador said: "I bring you good tidings of great joy, which shall be to all people. For unto you is born this day in the city of David *a Savior.*" That's what humanity needs.

Human beings have many problems. Who would begin to enumerate them? Some are hungry. Some are cold. Some are sad. They are sorrowing for the loss of a dear one. Some are sick. Some are brokenhearted. Some are lonely. Men have a lot of troubles and heartaches and problems. This is true the world over, even in these United States of America. But, my friends, there is one problem of the human race which has existed since the day when Adam and Eve fell into sin in Paradise and which has depressed human hearts more than any other, and that is the problem of a guilty conscience.

Adam and Eve had it, so they tried to run away and hide from God. Human beings have had it every day from that day unto this. And there is nothing which deals so harshly with man, which beats him down so fiercely, as does his guilty conscience. I wouldn't know any human being who has never had a guilty conscience. Sometimes I must deal with people who are very self-righteous, who would like to present themselves to me and to their fellow men, perhaps even to God, as individuals who are very good; but no one needs ever to be deceived by such a front, because the truth is that inside there still are stirrings which say to such an individual: "You old hypocrite, you know you are not that good. If people knew what kind of thoughts you think, what sort of sentiments arise out of your heart, they'd know how bad you are." And every human knows instinctively that even though he may be able to conceal things from his fellow men, he cannot conceal them from God. God knows all the time. And that's why people have such a sense of guilt. Ask any doctor, any psychiatrist. Ask the police officers and the judges. Ask parents, teachers, ministers. Why, ask yourself, and you will know what a guilty conscience does. It makes you burn with shame within. It fills you with a feeling of fear and awe and terror.

Christmas is so wonderful because Christ came to free us from that sense of guilt. He came to be our Savior. It was for this He came under circumstances of direst poverty. It was for this He grew up in a humble environment. It was for this He worked and suffered and died on Calvary's Cross, "the Lamb of God, which taketh away the sin of the world." It is very appropriate that behind the manger should stand the Cross. The two go together. The one lends meaning to the other.

JESUS SAVED EVERYBODY

No matter who you are, Jesus came for you. "I bring you good tidings of great joy, which shall be to *all* people." Write in your own name in this Christmas story. You will never understand it until you see your name printed on this sacred page and apply to yourself this Gift which God has sent. Oh, how I hope the Spirit of God will lay hold of each of your hearts, whether you be young or old, whether your sins be of the grossest and crudest nature, or whether they be of a more respectable and refined and, therefore, perhaps even more dangerous nature, the sins of the spirit: pride, self-righteousness, and so forth. I hope the Spirit of God will take hold of each of your hearts and let you see and feel that

Jesus is your Savior. Then you can have a good conscience. Then you can look God and the world in the eye, and with a firm step you can go through life, because your soul is at ease, your heart beats with joy, that sense of guilt is gone.

JESUS SAVES FROM FEAR

Jesus came also to free us from fear. You observe that the note of fear is right here in our Christmas story. "And, lo, the angel of the Lord came upon them [the shepherds who were upon Bethlehem's plains], and the glory of the Lord shone round about them, and *they were sore afraid.* And the angel said unto them, *'Fear not.'*" If you had been there, if I had been there, we would have been afraid, too. Our guilty conscience would have made us afraid in the presence of the holy ambassador of God. When you and I find ourselves in the presence of what is holy, we are afraid, because our conscience makes us afraid.

This plays into all parts of our lives. When we become ill, fear takes hold of us. When we have to go to the hospital for surgery, fear grips our hearts. If we find that we have to change jobs, we become filled with fear. If the newspaper headlines tell us about changes in economic circumstances, we begin to wonder, worry about tomorrow. As we grow older, we fear what might lie ahead. Will we suffer pain? Will we have a long, lingering illness? Will we be provided for? All manner of troublesome, worrisome questions begin to go through our hearts and minds. Fear is the common possession of the human family. And now God sends us His greatest Gift, frees our conscience and lets us realize that we, each day of our lives, enjoy the love of Him who sent His only-begotten Son.

It is to this love the human heart has responded. It is because of this love these beautiful carols of joy and lilting rhythm have been written for this day. It is because of this love that painters have been moved to put on canvas some of their loveliest artistic creations, as, for instance, the Madonna and the Child.

GOD'S GREATEST GIFT SHOWS HOW PRECIOUS MEN ARE IN GOD'S SIGHT

This day is a day of such joy because it gives us an understanding of how precious we are in the sight of God. After all, Christmas is for all people. That's what the angel said. That's how the Prophets had foretold it. The whole Bible bears witness to that one supreme truth. Jesus came for all. "God so loved *the world.*"

Sometimes you don't feel very important. Life seems to pass you by. You are so helpless over against the events of life. Often you cannot control the situations in your own home, to say nothing about the community in which you live, the industry in which you participate, or the world of which you are a citizen. When we begin to feel so small, so insignificant, when we think of the petty thoughts we have and the small things whereof we make ourselves guilty, we wonder how anybody can be concerned about us while the great, relentless march of time moves on and leaves us, as it were, at the side of the road. Whenever you are threatened with such an opinion of yourself, whenever it would appear to you as though you don't matter, then go to Bethlehem, and you will see how much you matter. You meant so much to God that in His love He sent the finest that He had, His only-begotten Son. That is the price tag which God has attached to you. It doesn't make any difference what your name is, how old or young, rich or poor, educated or uneducated, you may be. You see, this is what gives us our human dignity. This is what makes every human a precious being. That means first of all *you.*

But, by the same token, it means me, too, and all your other fellow men. Here in the Christmas story we learn how to regard our brothers and sisters in the human family. God thought enough of each one of them to send Christ for their redemption, Jesus, His only-begotten Son. The minute you catch that truth you will never again want to speak of any human being with contempt. You can never brush humans off as though they were of no significance. It will cut you to the quick to see one human being abuse another. It may be just a dirty, unwashed little urchin playing out there in the alley; it may be somebody with a coal-black skin; it may be some recent arrival from a foreign land who belongs to another nation and another race; it may be a man or woman so fallen, so lost, that men can see no hope for him, it all matters not. Inasmuch as it is a human being, it is one who in the eyes of God was precious enough to warrant the sending of Jesus for his salvation. You see, Christmas is a day of joy. It does have meaning.

JESUS RULES

Christmas is such a day of joy and Christ the one great unspeakable Gift also because this very day brings us an outlook on world affairs which should really comfort our hearts. The Christmas story does not start out in a very promising way, as you will have noticed each time you heard it. "And it came to pass in those days that a decree went out from Caesar Augustus that all the world should be taxed." Caesar Augustus was a Roman emperor. He was anything but a saint. The command which he gave was designed to squeeze some more tax dollars out of the masses of poor people in the Roman Empire. There was nothing pleasant or humanitarian about that. But see what happened. Caesar Augustus wasn't aware of it. He had no intention of playing a part with God in the accomplishment of any divine plans, and yet God used him. God overruled him. God turned what he intended purely as a kind of political business into divine channels, as it were, for because of the imperial decree Joseph and Mary also went to be taxed. God had said the Messiah was to be born at Bethlehem. Joseph and Mary were at Nazareth when the time came that she should be delivered; so God uses the command of Caesar Augustus to bring Mary to the place where the Christ Child should be born.

My friends, that's a wonderful fact. We are living in chaotic days. Many things are happening that might well disturb our minds and make our hearts fearful and restless. When we discover that hundreds of millions of people are on the march in India, in China, and in other parts of the world, that there are restless stirrings here and there and elsewhere; when we are apprised that there has been duplicity and treason in some of the highest and most confidential positions in our own Government, then we wonder what tomorrow will bring. But what can we do about it? We are so helpless. What can you and I do about it? How can we live happily, contentedly, quietly, and peacefully in such a world? It would appear as though we must awaken with a nightmare each passing night and arise to greet each new day with a heavy heart and a depressed mind.

Not so. It would be so if it were only for you and for me. But it isn't. Here you have it. God's hand is operative in history. Let the devil scheme as he may. Let the forces and hosts of evil plot as they like. Finally up and above and beyond them all is God, who loves us and who sent Jesus, God, who used Caesar Augustus, the mightiest man of his day, in order to accomplish His purposes for the salvation of mankind.

God still holds the reins of the universe in His hand, your God, who loves you. When you get up in the morning and you see that sun shining again, you say: "Look. How wonderful! Even as the sun shines anew, so the mercies of God are new for me today." And when you come to the end of a busy and troubled day and you lay your head down upon the pillow, you fall asleep as the arms of divine love embrace you. You say: "How wonderful! The angels of God are watching over me. The hand of God is ruling and guiding the destinies of nations. The Almighty will bend the wills and the hearts of the most wicked even to the fulfillment of His purposes. I can sleep peacefully, for God loves me, God watches over me, and God will accomplish for His ends what I cannot achieve." And so each day, because God sent Jesus and used a mighty emperor to accomplish His plans, you and I can live in peace and with joy and hope, with courage and confidence, pursue our tasks to the glory of God, who through His Son effected our salvation.

So when we think about these things and they penetrate a bit deeper into our hearts and souls and we begin to comprehend their significance a little more fully over against the cold, stern realities of life, we begin to realize why the angels were so happy, and we spontaneously join them in a beautiful song, "Glory Be to God on High."

The Meaning of Christmas

❖   ❖   ❖

Now I say that the heir, as long as he is a child, differeth nothing from a servant, though he be lord of all, but is under tutors and governors until the time appointed of the father. Even so we, when we were children, were in bondage under the elements of the world. But when the fullness of the time was come, God sent forth His Son, made of a woman, made under the Law, to redeem them that were under the Law, that we might receive the adoption of sons. And because ye are sons, God hath sent forth the Spirit of His Son into your hearts, crying, Abba, Father. Wherefore thou art no more a servant, but a son; and if a son, then an heir of God through Christ.—GALATIANS 4:1-7.

The spirit of Christmas is still all about us. We have once again commemorated the birth of our Lord. It is of utmost importance for each one of us now to take in the meaning which that event is to have for each of us.

FULFILLMENT OF HOPE

Our text reveals what that meaning is. When we read the Epistle for today, we discover first of all that the birth of Jesus represents the *fulfillment of hope*. Paul writes: "When

the fullness of the time was come, God sent forth His Son."
It would take many, many words indeed to describe somewhat adequately what those words "fullness of the time"
signify.

Ever since that dark and tragic hour in Paradise when man
fell into sin, God came to him with a promise that a Messiah
was going to come. This promise God repeated through the
mouths of His Prophets as the centuries slowly dragged on.
He gave a pictorial representation of the promise to His
people through the colorful religious ceremonies which He
prescribed for their use in the Temple at Jerusalem. All this
was done by God to prepare the hearts and the minds of
people for the coming of Jesus. But this was only a part of
the preparations which God made.

While He was telling men what they might look for, He
was at the same time setting the stage, if we may so speak,
for the appearance of the Christ Child. The great historical
events which came to pass during the days of the Old Covenant all were a part of these divine preparatory labors.

We can see the hand of God in history very clearly when
we go back to the fourth century before Christ and have a
look at the work and achievements of Alexander the Great.
Alexander came out of Macedonia with his Greek and Mace-
donian military forces. He marched triumphantly through
Asia Minor, down through Palestine, into Egypt and established the great city of Alexandria, which proudly bears his
name to this very day. Then he went eastward all the way to
the Indus River. He brought great areas under his imperial
control. Wherever he went, wherever he subjugated a people,
he established Greek colonies. He then already was aware of
the importance of "infiltration." He "sold" the ideas of the
Greek world to the conquered peoples by establishing Greek
colonies in their midst. These Greeks spoke the Greek lan-

guage. They lived in the Greek way. They adhered to the Greek ideas of life, culture, and government, and thus God, through the military conquests of Alexander, brought to the whole Mediterranean world one language, which in due course of time particularly the more cultured classes were to use as their common tongue. Thus God, who had promised a Savior, began to create a world in which the message of that Savior could be proclaimed to people everywhere by means of the most highly developed language humanity has perhaps ever known, the Greek language.

THE ROMAN EMPIRE

The days of Alexander were soon followed by imperial Rome. It wasn't too long before the Roman eagle began to spread his wings over an even greater part of the world, including that which once had fallen to the control of ambitious Alexander. When Rome found itself in possession of such vast territories and the governor of so many varied kinds of peoples and races, it was important for Rome to have a great network of roads by which military forces could be sped from one point to another wherever revolution might be brewing, wherever difficulty for the government might be threatening. And so all of this world was united, we might say, by a system of highways which made it possible for anyone who had a message to deliver to pass with reasonable facility and speed from one part to another and to tell people in that one known tongue, the Greek language, whatever he had to say.

Thus God set the stage for the coming of Christ. When the hearts and minds of men had been prepared and the dispersed Jews had carried the Messianic hope to the East, to the South into Egypt, to Asia Minor, to Greece and Macedonia, over into Italy and all the world, then "God sent forth

His Son, made of a woman, made under the Law, to redeem them that were under the Law." For centuries God had held up a beautiful hope. Many generations of people had come and gone, and many scoffers had said, "Nothing is happening." But the promises of God stand sure. When Jesus was born, it was true, as Phillips Brooks said: "The hopes and fears Of all the years Are met in thee [Bethlehem] tonight." God's promises found their most wonderful fulfillment.

GOD'S PROMISES ARE TRUE

My friends, you and I will never understand the real meaning of Christmas until we learn from this event to accept as true and real every promise that God has given. You know without my even telling you that God has given many precious promises to cheer your heart. He has invited you to pray. Jesus said: "Whatsoever ye shall ask the Father in My name, He will give it you." He has given you a blank check, put His name to it, and said: "Now you fill in the check. My signature is on it, and it's good." Well, it is good. If ever you have any doubts about it, remember how wonderfully God fulfilled the promise of a coming Messiah.

Probably there were those impatient souls who didn't think that God fulfilled His promises quickly enough. He didn't do it just as they thought He should. But in His own surpassingly wonderful way He did it. And so it is with the prayers which you address to God. He hears them; He hears every one of them, and in His own wonderful way will provide the answer. Whatever hope in your heart rests on the promise of God is a sure hope. It will never be dashed to pieces. It will never founder. It will never fail. It will find its fullest realization, and that reality is likely to be much more wonderful than anything you could ever even have pictured to yourself.

Jesus says: "Come unto Me, all ye that labor and are heavy laden, and I will give you rest." That's a comforting promise. You are acquainted with that promise, but probably there have been times when you haven't believed it. Maybe you have thought: Well, perhaps God has kept that promise with reference to other people, but He certainly is not keeping it in my case. Don't you ever believe it. When the hour comes in which you are inclined to doubt that promise, then think of the birth of Jesus. "When the fullness of the time was come, God sent forth His Son." That promise was fulfilled, and you will not understand the meaning of Christmas until you realize that God intends in the same wonderful way to keep every promise He has ever made. He is not going to fail you.

If your heart is heavy this morning, then build on His promise. He invites you to come. He does not intend to push you aside. In His own good way and day He will take care of you in such a marvelous manner that you will be ashamed beyond words for ever having questioned the truthfulness of the promise which He gave. Oh, God has given us many precious promises, and all of them are just as true as was the promise which He gave concerning the coming Messiah. Well, we must hasten on.

RELEASE FROM BONDAGE

When we read our text for today, we discover further that the birth of Jesus should make us realize that we *now are free people*. That is the meaning of Christmas. The coming of Jesus has effected our release. Our text uses rather strange language, which probably we don't grasp immediately. Paul says: "Now I say that the heir [he's thinking of the son of a rich man], as long as he is a child, differeth nothing from a servant, though he be lord of all, but is under tutors and governors until the time appointed of the father." In other words, Paul is taking a picture out of the world of his day. He says: When a rich man has a son, that son may be the prospective heir of everything the father owns; but so long as he is a child, he has no freedom to use these things. He lives under the control of tutors and nurses and governors and is really no different from one of the father's servants, and that condition will continue until the day appointed of the father. When the father says: "Now, my son, you have reached maturity; now you are no longer under the control of governors and tutors; now it is for you to live your own life; now you shall begin to enjoy what is your inheritance," then a day of freedom has come. Well, said Paul, that's the way it was with us spiritually. "Even so we, when we were children, were in bondage under the elements of the world. But when the fullness of the time was come, God sent forth His Son, made of a woman, made under the Law, to redeem them that were under the Law."

My friends, Paul is here talking about the very thing which lies at the heart of humanity's misery or happiness. When you understand what Paul is here saying and grasp its significance for your own soul, then you have laid hold of life's secret of happiness; and until you do, you will not know that secret. Paul had grown up under the Law. Paul had been taught from the earliest days of childhood that he had to do certain things in order to get right with God. So long as he failed to do those things with perfection, there could be no peace in his heart.

And you know, my friends, this, of course, is the unhappy situation in which humanity in its entirety finds itself. All over the world there are hundreds of millions of people who are trying to get right with God. It doesn't make very much difference how they do it, or what they think will be sufficient to satisfy the demands of their Creator. In some places they may think that placing a bowl of rice before an altar will help. In another place they may think that it will help if they write a lot of prayers upon little pieces of paper, form them into a wheel, tack this on the outside of the house so that the wind can spin these prayers around and thus waft them to the heavens. Elsewhere they may think of it more seriously and believe that it requires the sacrifice of their children or of their own lifeblood in order to work out a relationship of peace with their Maker. In the United States of America they may feel that it requires the giving of great sums to charitable purposes, or that it at any rate calls for an outward acceptance of a moral philosophy which revolves around the Golden Rule. But go where you will, to any people in any part of the world, in any time of the world's history, and you will find men laboring under this crushing burden, trying somehow to get right with God.

That was Paul's problem. He was enslaved to the Law. He was bound, trying and trying, but never really succeeding. You will all probably remember the account of the American aviator who became wedged in between broken parts of his wrecked plane. He could not move. There he lay. The hours went by, and the days went by. He had no food, no drink. It was impossible for him to get that crushing load off his body. It wasn't until some days later, when some other American boys happened by that way and found him, that he was released. Well, my friends, this pinned-down human being is a picture of mankind, of you, of me, of all men, of all ages, as we find ourselves hemmed in, held, and enslaved by the requirements of God's Law, which we are incapable of keeping.

And now Jesus has come. The one purpose for which He came was to release us, to get us out of that cramped position, and to give us freedom. Jesus has taken the burden of sin away, and we are free. You can't sigh a sigh of relief so deep and so prolonged as to express properly what has really happened to you by the coming of Christ. The whole load is gone. You are free. No longer need you go through life with agony in your soul, wondering day by day whether this is the day on which you are going to satisfy God or not. No, Jesus has redeemed you. He came to redeem them that were under the Law. That is the meaning of Christmas, and so now you are free.

In your relationship to God you are free. You don't go to church because you must. You come to church because you love to hear the story of your Savior's redeeming work. You don't give to church because you must. If that's the way you give, don't give. It hurts you to give when you give that way, and it doesn't bring any joy to the heart of the Savior at all. But if it is a delight for you to take of what God has given you and put it into the hand of the Savior and say: "Lord, use it for the good of my fellow men and for the upbuilding of Thy kingdom," then, you see, you are acting as a free, a liberated child of God.

THE POWER OF LOVE

When you go to work, you don't go to work because you must, whether you're a man who works at the assembly line, or a dentist filling teeth, or a doctor operating, or a teacher in the classroom, or a businessman behind the counter and the banking table. You don't do these things because you must. You don't keep your house clean and care for your children and prepare meals because you must. The "must" has been taken out of life. There is only one compelling power within you, and that is the power of love which says: "You want to do it—you want to do it—you want to make your life count—you want to show God how happy you are because of the fact that you have been released from the bondage of the Law."

If you employ people, you don't treat them like human beings and pay them adequately because you must. If you are a neighbor, you don't show kindness to the person next door who is sick and in trouble or in grief and sorrow because you must. You don't talk with respect about the Chinese over on the other side of the globe or about the poor Negroes in the jungles of Africa because you must. You do that because you are free. You do it because you want to do it, because the love that has come from Christ to you says: "Now, that's what you want to do. You want to do everything that will please this Christ and be in harmony with His holy will."

And so life has become an expression of freedom. You don't stay with your wife or your husband because you must. You don't care for and educate your children because you must. You don't pay your taxes and observe the laws because you must. You are a free child of God. You have been redeemed from the bonds of the Law and now are ready freely in love to live out your life. That's the meaning of Christmas. That's what Paul said. We were in bondage, "but when the fullness of the time was come, God sent forth His Son . . . to redeem them that were under the Law" so that we should have this freedom.

NEW RELATIONSHIP

And out of this now flows the fact that we then also enter into an altogether *new relationship with God*. Because we have been redeemed, "we now may receive the adoption of sons," says Paul. "And because you are sons, God hath sent forth the Spirit of His Son into your hearts, crying,

Abba, Father. Wherefore thou art no more a servant, but a son; and if a son, then an heir of God through Christ."

God, who sent Jesus, has sent the Spirit of God, who proceeds from the Father and the Son, to open your eyes, to let you look with understanding and appreciation upon the figure of Jesus. You now realize that you are free. You are redeemed. You can live your life no longer because someone holds a cudgel over your head, but because a fire of love is burning within your heart. Life becomes a free and blessed expression of love. And the Spirit of God, who brings you to that faith, now has you realize that there is no further dividing wall between you and your heavenly Father. You can look up to God and say, "Abba," which is the Hebrew for "Father." "Father"—that is the meaning of Christmas.

We are living in turbulent times. There is so much chaos in the world that one wonders from day to day just what is going to happen next, but your heart can be quiet. You don't have to suffer from the diseases of tension, so common in our time, because you're worried about the general situation. You have a Father, and you can trust in Him and commit yourself altogether into His gracious keeping and care. Every morning when you wake up, you can look up and say: "Father, I commit myself into Thy gracious keeping." And every night when you close your eyes and darkness surrounds you, you can say: "Father, I commit myself and all that I am and all that I have into Thy gracious care." That is the meaning of Christmas, to have this trust in the heavenly Father, and to know that because you are the Father's child, you are the heir of that Father. God is a good Father. It would be wonderful if we human fathers could be only a little more like Him in the fulfillment of our obligations. But however much we fail, He doesn't fail. He's generous. He gives us so much for every day that we can't begin to count His blessings.

But the generosity of today is as nothing compared with the full inheritance which is still awaiting us, which we shall have when we go to be with Him. Now we're making a journey. We're away from home, as it were. But when we get back home, He's going to swing the doors wide. He's going to put His arm around us and place a kiss of approval upon each of us. Then He will say to you: "My dear son, my beloved daughter, come, enter into all these glories which have been prepared for you." That is the meaning of Christmas. Christmas lifts hope beyond the uncertainties of our temporal experiences. Christmas gives us a hope that endures forevermore.

OUR RESPONSIBILITY

My friends, inasmuch as God has been good to each of us and revealed the meaning of Christmas to us, you and I should not find it difficult to realize that with this revelation and blessing goes a tremendous responsibility. After all, God has as much love in His heart for other people as He has for you. If God gives you something, He doesn't do it so that you should selfishly enjoy it and forget all the rest of the world. No, the only chance you really have for enjoying it is to share it. Isn't it strange how God has so fixed life that you can never enjoy anything just by yourself? God won't have it. No matter how you try, you're doomed to failure from the start. The only way you can enjoy anything that God has given you is to share it. That's a divine law, and it's just as sure as the fact that one and one are two.

We now, as the heirs of Christ, are to carry the spirit of Christmas into the lives of all our fellow men, so that what has come to bring light and cheer and hope into our souls may also bring the same blessings of God into their souls. This means that we have an assignment. In this critical hour of the world's history, we, as the children of God, the believers in Christ, have an assignment which calls for all that we through the power of the divine Spirit may be able to achieve. So, in the final analysis, the meaning of Christmas requires that you in life give expression to the truths of Christ and His love, both in your relationship to God and in your relationship to all of your fellow men.

May God grant that the fullest meaning of Christmas may work itself out in your heart and in your life.

A Cheerful Outlook

❖ ❖ ❖

But before faith came, we were kept under the Law, shut up unto the faith which should afterwards be revealed. Wherefore the Law was our schoolmaster to bring us unto Christ, that we might be justified by faith. But after that faith is come, we are no longer under a schoolmaster. For ye are all the children of God by faith in Christ Jesus. For as many of you as have been baptized into Christ have put on Christ. There is neither Jew nor Greek, there is neither bond nor free, there is neither male nor female; for ye are all one in Christ Jesus. And if ye be Christ's, then are ye Abraham's seed and heirs according to the promise.

GALATIANS 3:23-29.

The past year has poured its hours and its days into the sea of eternity. The new year lies before us as an unknown quantity. Going into a new year is somewhat like driving a car over an unknown country highway by night. We've all made the experience, I am sure, of having the illusion that the road is ending at the point where the rays of our headlights end. It always seems as though you were coming right to the end of the road because you can't make your vision penetrate beyond that point. The year ahead affects us somewhat that way because of its mysterious and unknown eventualities.

Each of us could ask a lot of questions this morning, questions for which each of us would like to have the answer. Is this year of our Lord going to be a year of prosperity or of want and adversity? I don't know. Is it going to be a year which will bring us good weather and good crops or bad weather and crop failures? I don't know. Is it going to be a year which will be marked by industrial peace or by industrial strife? I don't know. Is it going to be a year of good health or of prevailing plagues and epidemics? I don't know. Is it going to be a year of international peace or of worldwide war? I don't know. I can't answer these questions. You can't answer them. Truman or Taft, Wallace or Stassen, Stalin or Bevin, can answer them no more than you or I. So you see there are many, many aspects of life for which you and I would like to have an answer today as applying to the new year but for which no human can give an answer.

REASONS FOR CHEERFUL OUTLOOK

What does that mean? Does it mean that we must go into this new year with a sense of uncertainty? That we can proceed only with a glum spirit and with overshadowing clouds of gloom? No. Not at all, and thank God for it. If you and I read aright what we are told in the Epistle for today, then we understand that there are a number of very good reasons why you and I should proceed, with joyful outlook, to walk confidently and courageously into this new year of grace.

WE ARE CHILDREN OF GOD

The first reason which Paul mentions in our text is the fact that *we are the children of God*. Paul expresses it in this wise: "Before faith came, we were kept under the Law, shut up unto the faith which should afterwards be revealed. Wherefore the Law was our schoolmaster to bring us unto Christ, that we might be justified by faith. But after that faith is come, we are no longer under a schoolmaster. For ye are all the children of God by faith in Christ Jesus."

This language strikes us somewhat peculiarly. You and I wouldn't express ourselves in just these words. And yet the meaning of these words is not at all difficult to grasp. What Paul wanted to say was this. He and the Christians living in the Roman Province of Galatia, to whom he was writing, had at one time tried to work out the salvation of their souls by doing the things which God asked of them in His holy Law. They had, however, not succeeded in gaining the peace, for which they were striving. Because their lives were always marked by imperfection and moral, spiritual deficiencies, they never got that comfortable inner conviction that they were the children of God. The only thing the Law did for them was to convict them. No matter how hard they tried, the Law continued to say to them: "You are not God's children. You are sinners."

And then one day Jesus revealed Himself. Jesus presented Himself to Paul and, through Paul's preaching, to these converts of Galatia as the One who had saved them from their sins. Thus the Law had been a schoolmaster preparing their hearts, as it were, so that when Jesus appeared, they would recognize Him as the One whom they so sorely needed and accept Him as their one and only Hope. But now since Jesus had appeared unto them, since they had come to believe in Him as their Redeemer, they were the children of God. And, my friends, that is the thing you want to remember concerning yourselves.

As you stand on the threshold of a new year and all of the future lies out there shrouded in darkness and in mystery, you can still face it all with joyful outlook because you know that through faith in Christ you are a child of God. You can look up to the heavens and say, "Father." This means something. It means that no matter how mysterious the future may be and how deeply it may be hidden in secrecy, you can be fearless because you know that He who is the Creator of all, He who sustains life in everything that lives and breathes, He loves you. You are His dear son or His beloved daughter. He puts around you His arms, embraces you in His love, and says: "You are My child. Don't you be afraid." Just to know that He who sustains everything regards you as a member of His family and has a heart which overflows with infinite love in your behalf, that is the first reason our text would urge upon us why we should not let ourselves be disconcerted by the uncertainties of tomorrow, but rather stand firm at our place in life and go forward boldly. Indeed, God is our Father.

WE CAN WORK FOR A BETTER WORLD

Our text suggests a second reason why we should have a joyful outlook. God has thought not only of us. He has thought of all men, and in this lies a real reason for us to be happy and thankful. Paul put it this way: "Ye are all the children of God by faith in Christ Jesus. For as many of you as have been baptized into Christ have put on Christ. There is neither Jew nor Greek, there is neither bond nor free, there is neither male nor female; for ye are all one in Christ Jesus." If you and I could look out upon human society only through human eyes, if we had no special light which enabled us to see something which you can't see with mere human understanding, then the picture which is presented by the world on this January first would not be very encouraging. Round the globe hundreds of millions of people recognize the fact that there are now two gigantic nations standing opposite each other in the family of nations. One of these is the United States and the other the Union of Soviet Socialist Republics. The relationship between those two giants has not been a very happy one since the days of the war. Jealousy and suspicion have marked this relationship. Many are of the opinion that a war between these two nations, which, of course, would involve again all the other nations, is altogether inescapable.

Besides this particular relationship there are so many other unhappy relationships. Greece, China, India, the Holy Land are being torn by civil strife. In many other countries there is a process of social fermentation, the eventual outcome of which no man could be wise enough to foretell. So if you and I can see the world only as it can be seen through the eyes of man and human understanding, then we do not have a pretty picture upon which to look as of today, and from this particular vantage point in history.

But, again, let us thank God that this is not the only way in which we may look at human society. Paul knew another way, God's way, and it was by divine illumination that he could write: "There is neither Jew nor Greek, there is neither bond nor free, there is neither male nor female; for ye are all one in Christ Jesus."

JESUS SAVED ALL MEN

The Cross of Jesus is a mighty magnet. Jesus once said that if He were lifted up, He would draw all men unto Himself. When Jesus came into this world, He did not come only for a select group of Americans or a particular kind and class of Europeans. Jesus came for all. Jesus conceived of His Cross as a rallying point for all members of the human family. From all over the world, men, women, and children were to

be drawn to that Cross. There each of them should find, first
of all, peace with God, forgiveness for his sins, inner joy,
that sense of well-being that comes to a human when he
knows that all is well between him and his Maker.

The Cross, however, was not to serve only as a magnet
drawing all men unto itself, but it was also to serve as a
unifying force, the great leveling influence in human society
which wiped out all marks of distinction between kings and
beggars, between the educated and the illiterate, between
whites and blacks, Jews and Gentiles. Even though the world
of today presents to us a picture of division, opposition,
hatred, jealousy, strife, with the threat of a terrible war to
come, there is in the Cross of Christ a power which can
overcome all of these negative influences and unite human
hearts in the one family of God.

It is not true that you and I must accept the world where
we find it today. It is not true that there is no greater hope
for human society, and that all hope must be abandoned.
When you and I look back upon history for only 1,900 years,
we cannot but see what incredible progress has been made
in the improvement of social relationships. The world of our
day and the world of our Lord's day simply cannot be compared. No matter how pessimistic a person would like to be,
no matter how much he would like to assert that Christianity
has done nothing for the good of the human family, and no
matter how many arguments men might marshal to support
such a statement, the truth yet remains that the power of the
Cross of Jesus Christ in the affairs of men has been tremendous. It has effected changes for the better in the relationships of human beings such as people nineteen centuries ago
would never have dreamed possible. If such improvements
could be effected in the past, then who are we to say that

God has reached the end of His possibilities, that He can't do anything better than what He has accomplished up to this point. No, in this very fact that before the Cross of Christ all men can become united so that there is neither Jew nor Greek, neither slave nor freeman, neither male nor female, but all are one in Christ Jesus, our Lord, in that lies a promise for the possibilities of a better day.

OUR TASK

Obviously, you and I must not suppose that such a better day will come just by chance. If that day is to be ushered in, God would do so through the instrumentality of such influence as you and I can bring to bear in the living of our lives. Every now and then someone will say to me, "What can we do about it?" My friends, the answer is comparatively simple. Carrying out the answer is not so simple. If you want to know what you can do and what you should do in order to bring about a better world, you need but look at the things which Jesus required of the disciples whom He instructed and later on sent out into the world for that particular purpose.

First of all, be a Christian yourself, and live like a Christian. That sounds very simple. Unfortunately, it is not so easy. Simple, but difficult. The hardest thing you and I have to do in this world is to live like Christians. If you will take a good look at yourself, you will discover very quickly what a divergence there is between the standards of Christian living established by God and your own daily performance in life. Though we profess to be Christians, we think, we act, like the people who are not Christians.

Not only should we act like Christians, but we should talk like Christians. God has given us something to talk about.

While they who do not believe and who do not know the Lord Jesus have their topics of interest, you and I, as the sons and daughters of God, should have our peculiar and special topics of interest, chief of which should be the love of God in Christ. When we talk to other people about the things that God has done for our redemption, when we tell men what a beautiful and blessed thing it is to be a believer in Christ, then we are making our contribution toward the improvement of human society, because it is through this message another one and another one will be won for faith in Jesus Christ and changed into an obedient son or daughter of the heavenly Father.

Then, of course, all of us can and should pray. We're not nearly so helpless over against the world situation as we sometimes think we are. We think the only people who can do anything to influence world events are the people who sit in congressional halls or who gather with others for supposedly important international conferences. The fact that a poor invalid grandmother who sits in her invalid chair day after day, but who knows how to fold her hands and talk to God in prayer about the needs of her fellow men, that she may be having a vastly greater and more blessed influence for the good of human society than all of these supposedly mighty counselors, that is a truth we are all inclined to overlook and forget. You and I are not so helpless as others may think we are. We can and we should do something about bringing men together at the foot of the Cross.

WE HAVE AN ETERNAL HOPE

So we have reason to be joyful in our outlook upon the new year because we are the confident children of God and because we can do something about making this a better world in which to live. Paul would urge upon us one other reason why we should be joyful. He says: "And if ye be Christ's, then are ye Abraham's seed and heirs according to the promise." Let us suppose that it were possible for someone to stand up here this morning and tell you with all assurance that this year of our Lord was going to be a wonderfully prosperous year; that everybody would have an abundance of food and clothing; that everybody would be able to enjoy all of the fine material blessings which God has given us; that everybody would be well and healthy. Let us assume that such a promise could be made. Do you think that would suffice to put human hearts at rest, to make them feel easy? Not at all, because every human heart would realize: Well, that's this year. What about the next and the next? Let us assume that somebody could stand here and say: "For the next five, for the next ten, for the next twenty, fifty years, all is going to be well." Do you think that would put human hearts at rest? Not at all, because, in the final analysis, every human heart knows that beyond those years there is still an eternity that men must reckon with.

No human heart can be quiet unless it knows how to face eternity. And Paul would urge upon you this morning that your heart should be quiet because this whole eternity has been taken care of. Inasmuch as you are a son or daughter of God, you are an heir of God. You still have your greatest gifts of God waiting for you. The person who happens to be the child of a rich man may enjoy certain advantages during the father's lifetime, but that child will not come into the complete possession of his inheritance until the father has passed away and the estate is divided. You and I may enjoy countless gifts of God every passing day, and we do. But we do not come into the full inheritance of God's children until we step out of time into eternity. Fundamentally, the one reason why you and I need not be terrified by the uncertainties of tomorrow is that we have an insured inheritance waiting for us.

COMFORT AVAILABLE

It is a terrible thing when people don't have that outlook, that hope, upon which to rest. We have many occasions in life to call on people who have no hope for this world. It may be a person who is of advanced years. Why try to make this life or this world important to such a person when you know deep down in your heart that he hasn't very many more days to go? Perhaps you find yourself standing at the bedside of a man whose body is filled up with cancer. He may not know it, but you know it. Why stand there and say to such a man: "Oh, it will all be well. Don't worry. You're going to be healthy and in good shape again." You know it isn't true. Why lie to him? Just think what a terrible thing it is to find yourself face to face with such daily situations in life if all human hope ends with this little, fleeting earthly journey. But that isn't how it is. "If ye be Christ's, then are ye Abraham's seed and *heirs according to the promise.*"

And so, as you and I stand on the threshold of a new year, our hearts should be perfectly quiet. We are God's children. We may be very humble members of human society, but by the mercies of God we can do something about making this a better world by taking one man and another man, one child and another child, one woman and another woman, and bringing them with us to the foot of our Savior's Cross, where all become one in Christ. And, beyond all that, we have a glorious hope, the hope of a divine inheritance which shall satisfy our every want and fill us with an eternal light and peace and fullness of joy. And so it affords me real pleasure, as a minister of Christ, to say to you, on the basis of such truths as these: "May God grant to you and each of your dear ones a rich, happy, and blessed new year."

Is Christianity Worth the Price?

❖   ❖   ❖

Beloved, think it not strange concerning the fiery trial which is to try you, as though some strange thing happened unto you; but rejoice, inasmuch as ye are partakers of Christ's sufferings, that when His glory shall be revealed, ye may be glad also with exceeding joy. If ye be reproached for the name of Christ, happy are ye, for the Spirit of glory and of God resteth upon you. On their part He is evil spoken of, but on your part He is glorified. But let none of you suffer as a murderer, or as a thief, or as an evildoer, or as a busybody in other men's matters. Yet if any man suffer as a Christian, let him not be ashamed; but let him glorify God on this behalf. For the time is come that judgment must begin at the house of God; and if it first begin at us, what shall the end be of them that obey not the Gospel of God? And if the righteous scarcely be saved, where shall the ungodly and the sinner appear? Wherefore let them that suffer according to the will of God commit the keeping of their souls to Him in well-doing, as unto a faithful Creator.—I Peter 4:12-19.

The Epistle for today poses the question: Is Christianity worth the price? Peter was writing to the Christians in Asia Minor. He warned them: "Beloved, think it not strange concerning the fiery trial which is to try you, as though some strange thing happened unto you." Peter wanted the Christians of that day, as God wants all Christians of this day, to know that they must pay a price for being a Christian.

THE PRICE THAT MUST BE PAID

The Christians of Asia Minor were about to experience bitter persecutions. This was not because they had done something wrong. It was not because they had killed or stolen or in other ways transgressed the laws of the empire. This was wholly and solely because they were Christians, because they professed Jesus as their Lord and believed in Him as their Savior. That is why they were to experience the confiscation of their properties, the severing of family ties, the enslavement of their sons and daughters, and probably even the burning of their own bodies.

It may seem a bit irrelevant in this year of our Lord and in these United States of America to speak about the fact that you must pay a price to be a Christian, and yet it is not irrelevant at all. This holds true in every age and in every part of the world. It is true that some people who profess to be Christians never find out what it means to suffer as a Christian, because they do not take their Christianity seriously. An individual who professes to be a Christian but who lives like a worldling will never discover that there is a tension between Christianity and the world. Such an individual may pay lip service to Christ, but for all practical purposes he has deserted from the army of Jesus and joined the ranks of the worldlings. The world can see no difference between such a person and itself, hence the world has no bitterness toward any such individuals. But if you are a real Christian, then you will discover very quickly that you cannot be a follower of Jesus without paying the price for such discipleship.

You will discover that first of all you must fight a battle within yourself. Just to be a Christian means that there are always inner tensions between good and evil. This was what Paul meant when he said: "What I would, that do I not; but what I hate, that I do." And this is what Jesus meant when He said: "The spirit indeed is willing, but the flesh is weak." Paul fought all his life against the evil that was within himself. He always tried to lay hold of that perfect good, but he never quite reached it. This was a very painful and arduous struggle. Paul never could forget it.

Neither can you if you are determined to be a true follower of Christ and a genuine son or daughter of God. If you have earnestly tried to live as a Christian, then you will know how keen this battle is. A young man came into my study one day and said: "I am learning that there is nothing harder to do in this world than to live like a Christian from one Sunday to the next Sunday." This young man had seen the light, actually caught the spirit of what it meant to live like a Christian. The person who thinks that Christianity is easy has not caught its spirit. He doesn't know what the battle is all about.

THE STRUGGLE AGAINST SELF

If you are honest and look into your own heart, then you will know that many evil things arise from within you. You decide: "I am going to be unselfish. I am going to live a life of love. I will put my mind on things that are high and holy and noble." You form this determination within you, and you are sure you are going to carry it out. But as life moves on from hour to hour and from day to day, you discover again and again that your mind is occupied with mean and sordid things. You find within you attitudes of envy, selfishness, lovelessness, jealousy, bitterness, and the like. This is a constant struggle. No one can be a disciple of Jesus without paying that price. This is what the Apostle meant to say when he urged that each one must work out his own salvation in fear and trembling. So you cannot be a Christian without paying the price. You will undergo very severe trials within your own self, altogether separate and apart from all other experiences of life.

THE STRUGGLE AGAINST THE WORLD

Yes, the problem which you have with yourself will be a constant struggle from the cradle to the grave. But that is not all. If you are a true Christian, then you will also be separated from the world. Nominal Christians, as I have already stated, know nothing of this separation. They profess to be Christians and then adopt in full the ways and the philosophy of the unchristian, unbelieving world. Such people have no argument with the world, and the world has no argument with them. There is no conflict for them. Life apparently is very easy, but it is not so with the Christian.

The Christian workingman finds himself in a relationship of tension with the unchristian workingman. The Christian workingman has a respect for his employer. He believes that he should eat his bread in the sweat of his brow. He believes that he owes an honest day's work for an honest day's pay. He believes that it is his duty to do as much for his fellow men as he can, rather than to see with how little he can get by. When the Christian workingman presents himself thus to the world, he invites the ill will of his fellow workingmen who have a totally different philosophy of life.

The Christian businessman finds himself standing squarely against the businessmen who are not Christians. The Christian businessman thinks of himself as a steward of all that he possesses. He knows that the people who work for him are just as precious in the eyes of God as he is himself. He knows that he has a Lord and Master in heaven to whom he is accountable. He is desirous of sharing honestly, fairly, equitably, in the fruits of their labors with the people who work for him. Those who are not Christians do not have such a view. They think that kind of a businessman is a traitor to his own class. He is ruining things for them. He is spoiling the working people. He is setting up ideals that are too high. If he were greedy, if he were selfish, that they could understand. But that he should behave like a disciple of Jesus makes them angry.

YET OTHER TENSIONS

Husbands and wives who bear each other's faults and weaknesses, who in the spirit of love and forgiveness compose their difficulties, who patiently try to be helpful to each other, who think of the bond of marriage as a holy and lifelong bond, which can be properly severed only by death, are not liked by the world. Their very life stands as a reproach to a world which has no such regard for that which is holy and intended by God to be for the duration of life. There is a clear line of cleavage between the world and the Christians, and the world does not like the Christians' behavior and moral attitudes and ideals.

Young people, young men and young women, who are followers of Jesus and who have a sense of chastity and decency are not liked by the dissolute worldlings, who have no such ideals of conduct. The young men and the young women who want to live unclean lives and satisfy their carnal lusts are reproached by the very life and existence of Christian young men and young women; so they do not like them. They despise them as prudes. A Christian cannot live in this world without having tensions between himself and the world. A Christian is in perpetual conflict with the world because of the very things he believes.

Why were those Christians in Asia Minor, which, as you know, now is Turkey—why were those Christians persecuted? They could have prevented it very easily. Had they been ready to burn a little pinch of incense to the Roman emperor, they would not have been persecuted. Had they been willing by this simple little gesture to recognize the divinity of the Roman emperor, their lives would have been perfectly serene and secure as far as Roman armies and jailers were concerned. But they could not do that. These Christians said: "No. We have one Lord, Jesus Christ. We cannot give divine honor to a man. This belongs to our Lord and Savior." This faith distinguished them. They could not have held that faith if they would have said: "Caesar is our lord, too, and the mystery religions and those gods and goddesses who are worshiped in this pagan temple are all right. We have nothing against them." Had they said this, then there would have been no enmity against them on the part of the world. But because they said: "No, there is only one Lord," that is why the world hated them. That is why their properties were taken away from them and their lives were destroyed.

THE WORLD'S ATTITUDE UNCHANGED

The world still has no use for people who say: "There is only one Lord." The world does not mind those people who say: "Well, I believe in Jesus, but there are many different ways in which people live out their lives. I am broad about things like that." Why should anybody quarrel about that kind of religion? But it is quite different when Christians say: "No, there are not a half-dozen great religions in this world, all of equal merit. There is only one way in which you can be saved, and that is by grace, through faith in Jesus Christ. It was Jesus who said: 'I am the Way, the Truth, and the Life, no man cometh unto the Father but by Me.' So I cannot approve of these other religions. I must disapprove of them. This is *the* religion and no other." The world does not like that. Then the world says: "That is narrow. That is bigoted." There is no affection in the heart of the world for a disciple of Jesus.

So you, even in this year of our Lord, in these United States of America, must not expect to go through life as a Christian without experiencing fiery trials. It is not probable that you and I are going to be thrown into jail for our faith, because Christians are quite numerous in this country, and they do exercise quite an influence, at least from a civic point of view. We are quite secure. Some folks fear that Russian influence may become so dominant still in our lifetime that even you and I may experience the kind of things that the earliest Christians experienced. Well, none of us knows. God has hidden such things from our eyes. Certainly, it would be pessimistic to think that such a thing will happen in our lifetime. I would not say that it could not happen in the United States of America. Even so, we cannot, despite all of that, go through life without a struggle, without these fiery trials. Sometimes physical suffering is easier to bear than scorn and mockery and contempt and cold indifference. When people just shove you aside as though you didn't count in human society, as though they wrote you off completely, that is very hard to bear. Christians often find that extremely difficult to contend with.

The question is: Is it all worth the price? Why should we expose ourselves to the scorn of the world? What are we as

Christians getting out of it? What does it all mean and lead to?

IT'S A BATTLE FOR ETERNAL VALUES

Peter thought it was eminently worth while. He said not only: "Bear your sufferings," but also: "Rejoice, inasmuch as you are partakers of Christ's sufferings." He wanted his readers to be sure that they would not suffer because they had violated the laws and made themselves subject to legal punishment; but if they could suffer for Jesus, if they could be identified with Christ in this battle against evil, then they should count themselves highly honored because of the privilege. This is the way the Spirit of God would have you look at your battle for Christ, at this struggle that goes on within you. What a glorious battle! That is the real battle of life.

Here is the Spirit of God and the love of Jesus Christ implanting a new power and new ideals in life and enabling you to take up the battle and to stand with Jesus on your side. You fight day by day against all that is evil within you.—You struggle by prayer, by reading the Word of God, by hearing the Word of God, by receiving food for your soul at the Lord's altar. You strengthen yourself by doing that which is good. You go on day by day, trying again and again to attain to some higher degree of moral achievement. You see the example of Jesus, and you try to emulate it. You fall by the wayside, and the Spirit of God takes hold of you, lifts you up, and you try again.—What a marvelous battle! Has there ever been anything more challenging to a human being than a struggle like that? When you are engaged in that struggle, that is a fiery trial. That is truly worth while. Oh, men think it is wonderful when they adventure for the gaining of money or fame. They think that is something whereof to be proud.

To this they devote all their wits and their energies. Still, my friends, here is a battle that is infinitely more worth while. Here is a battle for things that are ultimate, the eternal, the holy, the spiritual. So this struggle, this Christian battle, is worth while.

IT'S A STRUGGLE FOR GREAT SOCIAL VALUES

And likewise the fiery trial is worth while which grows out of the tensions existing between the children of God and the unbelieving, God-estranged world because of a different social outlook. What are we proud of as human beings? Are we proud of the slums? Are we proud of the streets that are lined with brothels? Are we proud of the haunts and dens of vice which cater to the drunkards and the prostitutes and to the degenerates of life? Are we proud of wars? Are we proud of the great devastated cities of many countries? Are we proud of the hungry, the cold, and the homeless? Are we proud of those who have no regard for the holiness of marriage or the sanctity of childhood or the preciousness of human beings? No, those are not the things we are proud of.

The only things in human history whereof we can truly be proud are the things that rise out of the love of Jesus Christ. We are proud as human beings of the view of life which has a profound respect for the sacredness of the individual human because he was created by God and redeemed by Jesus Christ and is intended for a heavenly home. We are proud of all those agencies of mercy which minister to the poor, the destitute, the aged, the sick, the orphaned. We are proud of the manifestation of justice and of humanity in the administration of government or in the affairs of business as carried on by Christian men and Christian women. These are the things of which we are proud.

Even the worldling cannot be proud of what he does. The

devil may lure him into the doing of evil things; but once he has done them, he is filled with despair and overcome with shame. He has nothing whereof to speak. If he wants to be a member of human society and lay hold of some of the glory that may belong to man, he must point to the things that have been done in the name of God and in the spirit of Jesus Christ. So, you see, this battle between good and evil, this struggle of the Christian over against the world, is eminently worth while. The trials may be fiery. You may have to pay a great price for being a son or a daughter of God, but the price is worth paying.

OUR CHALLENGE

So, here, then, is a challenge for all of us. We are on the threshold of a new year. The days will unfold themselves by the mercies of God as time moves on. We do not know what will come to us individually or collectively from day to day, but here is a call of God to take up the battle, to stand firmly and foursquare as sons and daughters of His, as followers of His, as believers in the Redeemer, who will fight evil within them and evil without them.

Here is something that calls for the most heroic in husband and wife, in father and mother, to keep evil out of the sanctity of their home. Fight it as you would fight the devil himself. Here is a call to the workingman, to the businessman, to accept the challenge, to shun all that is evil, and to say: "As God gives me strength in this kind of world, I am going to live as a Christian." Here is a call to the poet to use his imagination and to put into dramatic forms and words the great ideals so as to inflame men with these ideals and to call them to the service of God and of Jesus Christ. Here is a call to the Christian teacher who has the boys and the girls, the young men and the young women, the citizens and bur-

den-bearers of tomorrow, sitting before him day after day
to inspire them, to kindle within them the fires of passionate
devotion to Jesus, to have the courage and the confidence to
bear the fiery trials with complete assurance that only victory
awaits the children of God. Here is the call to the Christian
pastor time and again to mount the pulpit and to extend the
sweet Word of divine truth and forgiveness, to invite young
and old, men and women alike, rich and poor, to invite them
all, to come and enlist under the banner of Jesus Christ and
to fight, knowing that they are the light of the world, the salt
of the earth, and that through them God would bring blessings to all other men.

I hope the Spirit of God will use this little study of a
beautiful and challenging text in such a way that you will
catch something of its meaning, that you will learn how to
take your Christianity more seriously, recognize the battle
that is to go on within and without. I hope God will let you
understand how significant you are as a potential benefactor
of the human race, as a Christian. Then this year of grace will
be for you a marvelous adventure for God and for men.

May the Lord in His mercy grant this to each of us for
Jesus' sake. Amen.

Light! Let It Shine!

❖   ❖   ❖

Arise, shine; for thy light is come, and the glory of the Lord is risen upon thee. For, behold, the darkness shall cover the earth and gross darkness the people; but the Lord shall arise upon thee, and His glory shall be seen upon thee. And the Gentiles shall come to thy light and kings to the brightness of thy rising. Lift up thine eyes round about, and see. All they gather themselves together, they come to thee. Thy sons shall come from far, and thy daughters shall be nursed at thy side. Then thou shalt see and flow together, and thine heart shall fear and be enlarged, because the abundance of the sea shall be converted unto thee, the forces of the Gentiles shall come unto thee. The multitude of camels shall cover thee, the dromedaries of Midian and Ephah. All they from Sheba shall come. They shall bring gold and incense, and they shall show forth the praises of the Lord. All the flocks of Kedar shall be gathered together unto thee, the rams of Nebaioth shall minister unto thee. They shall come up with acceptance on Mine altar, and I will glorify the house of My glory. Who are these that fly as a cloud and as the doves to their windows? Surely the isles shall wait for Me, and the ships of Tarshish first, to bring thy sons from far, their silver and their gold with them, unto the name of the Lord, thy God, and to the Holy One of

Israel, because He hath glorified thee. And the sons of strangers shall build up thy walls, and their kings shall minister unto thee; for in My wrath I smote thee, but in My favor have I had mercy on thee. Therefore thy gates shall be open continually; they shall not be shut day nor night, that men may bring unto thee the forces of the Gentiles and that their kings may be brought. For the nation and kingdom that will not serve thee shall perish; yea, those nations shall be utterly wasted.—Isaiah 60:1-12.

LIGHT NEEDED

Our text speaks of light, as you will have observed. Light—that is the one thing which the world of our day needs. Some folks may not think so. Some like to speak of our age as the "age of enlightenment." Viewed from a certain point of view, it may be justly so called. It is a fact that in many spheres of human interest we have made more progress in our day than did any other age. We know today how to prevent epidemics of smallpox, diphtheria, yellow fever, malaria, and other diseases. We know today how to annihilate time and distance by our modern methods of communication and transportation. We know today how to produce en masse through the great assembly lines of our vast industrial enterprises. We even know a little more about the inner workings of man through the studies of psychology and psychiatry. We have gained somewhat deeper insights into the significance of human relationships through our study of sociology. And yet it remains a fact that ours is an age of darkness.

DARKNESS PREVAILS

When Isaiah said in his own beautiful and dramatic way: "For, behold, the darkness shall cover the earth and gross darkness the people," he might well have been looking twenty-seven hundred years into the future and talking about the very day in which you and I are living: for with all of the things which we have discovered in our workshops and laboratories, we have not yet learned how through the power and ingenuity of man we can change man into a finer, nobler creature. We have learned how to split the atom and how to control and use atomic energy, but we have not learned how we can so change the human heart that atomic energy will be used for the good and not for the destruction of mankind. We may be more conscious of social problems and difficulties in our day than were generations of the past, but we do not know how we can make white people, black people, Jewish people, Gentile people, live alongside one another in a spirit of peace and mutual esteem. We do not know how we can make those who do the employing and those who are employed recognize mutual responsibilities and live each for the other instead of against each other. Although we probably have the most learned, the most carefully schooled statesmen the world has ever known, yet the finest and the most brilliant among them, drawn from the great and small nations of the earth, do not know how to get one nation to live in a relationship of peace with another nation. What is more, the wisest of men do not know how to bring peace, real, honest peace, into the heart of any individual.

The earth is covered with a very black cloud of darkness, and the world needs light. Because that is true, many hearts are filled with fear. That is why terror has gripped the soul of humanity. Read what men are saying in their books, their essays, their poetry, as published in our day, and you will discover that all of them are haunted by black fear. "Darkness shall cover the earth and gross darkness the people." That was what Isaiah said, and that is what holds true in this our day. The fact that it is so, that greed and lust, selfishness and cruelty, vice and irresponsibility, are dominant is manifested in many ways.

The breaking and disintegrating homes of our time show the heartlessness of human beings. Yesterday afternoon I stood at the bedside of a little girl, five and a half years old, who was to be taken off to another hospital for a very serious operation tomorrow morning. She's one of our little kindergarten children, and you may remember her in your prayers. I said to her, "Who is your best friend?" She said, "My mamma." I said, "Have you any other?" She said, "Yes, my daddy." Of course, I wanted her to say, "Yes, Jesus." But she first thought of those who were the representatives of Jesus to her. Think how many boys and girls five years old, a little older or a little younger, would love to say, "My best friend is my daddy, my mamma," and they haven't a mamma or a daddy of whom they can say it, not because these are not living, but because they have abandoned their own flesh and blood. There is no child so young nor so old but it wants to be able to say, "My best friend is my mamma, my daddy." The cruelty and the selfishness of the human heart is manifesting itself in this particular area of life in a most terrifying way. The general looseness of living, excessive eating and drinking, and general dissipation, crimes of an unblushing nature, are so common in our time, and the dominance of sin, the low-hanging, black, heavy cloud of darkness, is so obviously present that anyone with any moral sensibilities at all must realize that "darkness covers the earth and gross darkness the people."

LIGHT IS AVAILABLE

All of this would be very tragic if that's the way it had to be, but it is all the more tragic because it doesn't have to be that way. There is light, and our text speaks of that light. That light does not come out of the laboratories of men, but it comes through the mercies and the goodness of God. Isaiah says: "Thy light is come, and the glory of the Lord is risen upon thee. . . . The Lord shall arise upon thee, and His glory shall be seen upon thee." Isaiah is talking of those who know God and the Christ of God: then, the promised Messiah; today, the Messiah who has come.

The love of God has broken through the heavy, black clouds of sin. God has come into human flesh in the person of His Son, has identified Himself with man for the purpose of dissipating the clouds of darkness and letting the light of divine love shine into the hearts and souls of His sons and daughters here below. This is a wonderful story—how God came, how He broke through and in the person of a little Child revealed Himself. Jesus grew up into manhood. He assumed the responsibilities of His office as the Savior of mankind. Every word He uttered, every deed He did, was expressive of love. It was in the life of Jesus that God opened up the door to His heart, so that every human being should be able, through the ministry of Christ, through the character and nobility of His life and love, to realize what it looks like in the Father heart of God. If you want to know how God feels toward you, you need only look at Jesus and see how He dealt with men. When you see His love, then you see the love that is in God's heart for you.

Jesus went on. He took upon Himself the guilt of the human family. He suffered as men should have suffered. He died instead of those who should have died, and He arose again. He brought light. Here is the light of the love of God which says to each individual soul: "You are redeemed. You need not despair in your sins, because they have all been atoned for. Don't let sin drive you on. Don't feel that you are so wound about by the web of evil and iniquity that you cannot be freed from it. Jesus has freed you. Put your faith in Him. Trust in Him. He has redeemed you not only from the guilt of sin, but also from the power of sin. You don't have to be a helpless slave of your weaknesses. You don't have to be pulled along helplessly by the temptations of a world estranged from God. You don't have to be destroyed by your lust for that which is wrong and contrary to the will of your Maker. Trust in God. Rely upon the love of Jesus. Accept the power of His Holy Spirit. Fight and pray, and you can be free. You can live a good life. You can be a noble son or daughter of your heavenly Father. There is light. Light is there to dissipate darkness. Life should not be an existence in unrelieved gloom in which we stumble along from evil to evil only to find ultimately our own destruction. Life should be an upward path that is illuminated by the love of God and that leads us on to greater heights of moral victory in this life, to profounder insights into spiritual truth, and to ultimate perfection in the presence of Him who died to save us from all that is evil. There is light.

THE LIGHT MUST BE SPREAD

But obviously this light is not going to benefit men unless they are aware of it. This light was not brought into the world for the purpose of putting it under a bushel, and so Isaiah got busy to tell men about this light. That's why he preached sermons like this and proclaimed these great and wonderful truths. And this now is the privilege and the responsibility which God lays upon everyone who has found the light, "Arise, shine."

Isaiah says to the Church, "Arise, shine, for thy light is come." This, my friends, is the business of the Church, to be the dispenser of light, to let the light of God's love radiate into the remotest parts of the world. It was never the plan of Jesus that the light of divine love should be limited to just a small sphere of humanity. The light of divine love was intended not only for churches built along Gothic lines and called houses of worship. This light is to penetrate to the remotest parts of the earth. It is to go into the palace and into the hovel. It is to go into the great industries of this and other countries. It is to find its place in every nook and cranny of human life and interest. Wherever there are men, this light of God's love should go. And it is your job, as one of the enlightened of God, to bring that light. "Arise, shine."

How does that strike you? If you believe that the world is in darkness and if you believe that the love of God in Christ is the only light that can dissipate that darkness, what are you doing personally as an enlightened individual to spread that light? The message of that love is to be preached. The message of that love is to be taught. That love is to be witnessed to by all who have experienced it in their own hearts. No one who is a follower of Jesus and who has the light of the Gospel in his own soul has the right to withhold that light from anyone else. If it be true that the world is in darkness, that there are literally hundreds of millions of people whose souls are crying out to they know not what, but still crying out in hopeless despair, doesn't that affect your heart at all? Doesn't it hurt you to see people walking in darkness, throwing their lives away in sin, in dissipation, in drunkenness and transgressions of one kind or another? What are you doing so that the light of God's love may come into those lives?

You see, I couldn't think about a text like this without trying to evaluate what is happening in our church. How many of our people are really putting their hand to the plow? How many of our people are trying earnestly to help pro-

mote the program of Jesus Christ, to bring this message out
to that world that is lost in darkness? After all, the number
of interested workers is comparatively small. So many go
their way. They have the Gospel, and that's all they are
concerned about. They never yet have heard the Lord say,
"Arise, shine." They've never heard Jesus say, "You are the
light of the world." You see, in the face of the world's darkness and God's light, there is no way in which anyone can
excuse himself from an active participation in the spreading
of that light. I hope that every family here represented will
make it a matter of family consideration and discussion to
ask themselves: What are we doing? Are we helping to build
the Kingdom of God? Are we helping to teach this Word?
Are we active, aggressive witnesses for Christ? Or do we act
as though it all didn't mean anything to us?

SOME MAY PREFER DARKNESS TO LIGHT

Sometimes folks try to excuse themselves from active participation by saying, What's the use? It isn't going to do any
good anyhow. Well, a great many things could be said about
that particular subject, but it does remain a fact that not all
the people who hear the Gospel are going to accept it. Isaiah
was aware of that. It is tragic when people hear it and don't
accept it, because the consequences are terrible. This is what
he said: "For the nation and the kingdom that will not
serve thee shall perish; yea, those nations shall be utterly
wasted." If ever there has been a generation of people which
should have the capacity to understand the truth of those
words, it ought to be ours. We have lived through two bloody
world wars. We have seen what indescribable heartache,
suffering, and destruction can come to people when they turn
from God and when God in His judgment allows the scourge
of war to come upon them.

Countries most widely devastated have been among the countries once most richly blessed with the Gospel. No country in the world has had a better opportunity to turn to Christ, to live in the light of God's love, than did the German people. And yet very many of them turned their backs on the light of God and chose to live in gross darkness. Though the revelation was in their midst, they would not accept it. Their rejection, however, has cost them dearly, and today many of them are groping, trying to get out of darkness back to light. In our bulletin for today appears the name of one of the most prominent churchmen of Germany. It was my privilege to have a private interview with him for about a half hour and to show him our church and also to hear one of his addresses. It is really pitiful to see how the poor people for whom he is the spokesman are trying to meet the needs of the hour.

Even professing Christians in our country, or should I say in Grace Church, don't seem to understand that no people can reject God and the light of Christ without bringing upon itself the judgment of God. I'm sure that if every business and professional man, every employer and working man and woman, in Grace Church understood and believed that the whole well-being of America will be determined by our attitude to the light of God's love in Christ, then they would work with might and main to spread that light. But somehow even some professing Christians seem to think that it isn't so important and that somehow we in America can go on and content ourselves with our economic wealth, with the ease and comfort amidst which we live and which we enjoy. We seem to think this will always go on, no matter what we do about spreading the light and no matter what America does about accepting the light.

There have been Christians who had a finer insight. Some of the fathers in the early days of our country understood this. This is what Daniel Webster said: "If we abide by the principles taught in the Bible, our country will go on prospering; but if we and our posterity neglect its instructions and authority, no man can tell how sudden a catastrophe may overwhelm us and bury all our glory in profound obscurity."

Daniel Webster knew what the Bible had to say on this particular subject. So it is for us to make our choice. You and I, as the enlightened sons and daughters of God, can help our country get light, or we can go our own way and busy ourselves with the little physical, material, and social things of life and neglect the great spiritual issues and see our own country and the country of our children and children's children go down to an inescapable doom.

MANY WILL APPRECIATE TRUE LIGHT

Yes, it is true, not all those who hear the Gospel will accept it, but Isaiah wasn't a pessimist. This is one of the most heartening passages in all the Scriptures. Will you let me read it to you again? He says: "Arise, shine; for thy light is come, and the glory of the Lord is risen upon thee. . . . The Lord shall arise upon thee, and His glory shall be seen upon thee." And then what will happen? "And the Gentiles shall come to thy light and kings to the brightness of thy rising. Lift up thine eyes round about, and see: All they gather themselves together, they come to thee. Thy sons shall come from far, and thy daughters shall be nursed at thy side. Then thou shalt see and flow together, and thine heart shall fear and be enlarged, because the abundance of the sea shall be converted unto thee, the forces of the Gentiles shall come unto thee." Then he turns to this Oriental imagery: "The multitude of camels shall cover thee, the dromedaries of Midian and Ephah. All they from Sheba shall come. They shall bring gold and incense, and they shall show forth the praises of the Lord. All the flocks of Kedar shall be gathered together unto thee, the rams of Nebaioth shall minister unto thee. They shall come up with acceptance on Mine altar, and I will glorify the house of My glory. Who are these that fly as a cloud and as the doves to their windows? Surely the isles shall wait for Me, and the ships of Tarshish first, to bring thy sons from far, their silver and their gold with them, unto the name of the Lord, thy God, and to the Holy One of Israel, because He hath glorified thee. And the sons of strangers shall build up thy walls, and their kings shall minister unto thee; for in My wrath I smote thee, but in My favor have I had mercy on thee. Therefore thy gates shall be open continually, they shall not be shut day nor night, that men may bring unto thee the forces of the Gentiles and that their kings may be brought."

Isaiah wasn't a pessimist. He didn't think that the Gospel of Jesus Christ was going to be preached in vain. He didn't believe that the light of God's love would shine without finding its reflection in the hearts of men. He saw a beautiful picture. From all over the world, people were going to come, and not only people of Israel, to which he belonged, but Gentiles.

There was Another who had a great vision. He wasn't a pessimist either. He said: "And I, if I be lifted up from the earth, will draw all men unto Me." Jesus didn't think that He was going to die in vain. He had a wonderful picture of the masses of people that were going to come. So, my friends, you and I who have received light from the Spirit of God, whose hearts are comforted and strengthened, inspired and cheered by the truth of God's love, God's forgiving mercy and grace, should give ourselves to this task, confident that it will not be done in vain, that Jesus, who let a star shine to the Wise Men of the distant East, died for all, and that His own are to be found everywhere. And as we allow that light to shine forth, it will attract men, and they will come. There is darkness, but the dark clouds have been torn by the light of God's love. There is hope, and it is for you and me to carry the light of hope out into the world so that it may be shared by our fellow redeemed.

I hope the Spirit of God will use this meditation on this beautiful text from Isaiah to make all of us more zealous, vigorous bearers of light.

God's Plea

❖   ❖   ❖

I beseech you, therefore, brethren, by the mercies of God, that ye present your bodies a living sacrifice, holy, acceptable unto God, which is your reasonable service. And be not conformed to this world; but be ye transformed by the renewing of your mind, that ye may prove what is that good and acceptable and perfect will of God. For I say, through the grace given unto me, to every man that is among you, not to think of himself more highly than he ought to think; but to think soberly, according as God hath dealt to every man the measure of faith. For as we have many members in one body and all members have not the same office, so we, being many, are one body in Christ and everyone members one of another.—ROMANS 12:1-5.

GOD PLEADS IN LOVE

If you can forget that I am here, I am sure it will prove help-ful. Try to imagine yourself as standing in the presence of Almighty God. Imagine that God is talking to you directly. He has a message. He wants to plead with you. He wants to do it in a very kind and gentle way. He says, "I beseech you." He is eager that you, professing to be His children, should behave like His sons and daughters.

He wants to impel you to heed His plea because of the love which He has for you. "I beseech you, therefore," He said when He first uttered this plea through the mouth of the Apostle Paul, "I beseech you, therefore, brethren, by the mercies of God." God doesn't talk down to you. God doesn't hold a club over your heads. He is not trying by force to drive you into something, but He is appealing to you. He wants you to remember how good, how gracious, how merciful He has been to you. He wants you to recall that He sent Jesus into this world, His very finest Gift, His dearest and most precious Treasure, His only-begotten Son, to save you. He wants to say to you: "Don't you remember that I do you good each passing day? The food you eat, the clothing you wear, the shelter which protects you, the home whose love is yours, your dear ones, your friends, I give them to you. The opportunity which you have every day to do something worth while, to be of benefit to your fellow men and to find satisfaction for your own heart, is My gift to you. Your health, your ability to enjoy music, to thrill to the rhythm of poetry, all these things I give you every passing day. Now, because of these mercies, I plead with you, behave like My sons and daughters. I am your Father. You belong to My family. Live as My sons and daughters ought to live."

GOD PLEADS FOR A LIVING SACRIFICE

"Well," you say, "God, that is all correct and true. You are kind to me. You are very gracious to me. What do You want me to do to live like Your child?" And God gives you the answer. He says, first: *"Present your bodies a living sacrifice, holy, acceptable unto God, which is your reasonable service."* These words were written to the Christians at Rome. These poor people lived in a terrible social environment. You have all heard enough about Roman history to remember that the

Roman people in Christ's day lived very wicked lives. They were given to wild excesses. Drunkenness and gluttony, adultery and licentiousness, were a part of their daily lives. They were beginning to destroy the very foundations of their society. They were hastening the day when the Roman Empire was to crumble because it had rotted away at the core. What they wanted was bread and circuses. They wanted to be delighted by bloody spectacles in the arena. They conceived of their bodies as instruments for sin. And the Christians were surrounded by such people. So God pleaded with His children living in this great world metropolis: "Don't you do as they do. Present your bodies as living sacrifices."

Could any plea be more timely for God's children living in these United States of America in this year of our Lord than this plea? The news of today is made up in no small part by accounts of cocktail parties, excessive, immoderate feasting, adultery, obscenity of one kind or another. As a matter of fact, the situation is so bad that the very people who make a profession of reporting gossip about entertainers in night clubs and on the stage of the American theater sicken of it themselves. If you follow the critical comments of such writers, you will know whereof I am speaking. Think of it! The other day one of the best-known theatrical figures of America died. Every newspaper and news magazine in the country told the sad and tragic story of how this man gloried in his excessive use of intoxicating liquors. The greatest and the most interesting thing they could say of him was that he was a drunkard who had killed himself by his manner of living. Think of it! People who occupy high places and earn vast sums of money with comparative ease and the people in low places who slave from Monday morning until Saturday noon to get a few dollars vie with one another as to how they are going to spend it in satisfying carnal lusts. This morning, as you stand face to face with your Creator, He, your Father, wants to say to you: "Don't you do that. You are My children. Live as My sons and daughters ought to live. Present your bodies a living sacrifice, acceptable unto God. Remember, your bodies were not intended to be tools for sin and licentiousness, but they were intended to be a temple for the Holy Spirit, who would dwell within you."

GOD PLEADS FOR A TRANSFORMATION

Continuing His plea, your Father would say to you this morning: "*Be not conformed to this world, but be ye transformed by the renewing of your mind, that ye may prove what is that good and acceptable and perfect will of God.*" The power of the world has always been strong over God's children. When the Children of Israel were in the Babylonian Captivity, they were profoundly affected by the paganism, the idolatry, and the immorality of the Babylonian people. The Christians who lived in the city of Rome, or Corinth, or Ephesus, or Antioch were all being influenced by the spirit of the world which surrounded them. God knows that. He knew it then, He knows it now. That was why He had Paul plead with the Christians of that time not to conform themselves to the world's way of thinking and living.

The power of the world has never been greater than it is today. I think it is correct to say that boys and girls who are still in grammar school know more about the world today and about its ways than did the average experienced adult of some few decades ago. The daily press, the radio, the movie, the billboards, all serve to bring the ideas of the world to the attention of everyone. Even children who can only page through a magazine and see the advertising pages and the pictures which are there presented get an idea as to how the world thinks, what the world believes. Never in all history has the world had an opportunity to influence God's children in its direction as it has today. So if it was important for God to plead with the Christians at Rome nineteen hundred years ago, "Don't conform yourselves to the world," that plea is vastly more important today.

God says not only: "Don't conform yourselves to the world," but also: "Be ye transformed by the renewing of your mind." God wants you as His sons and daughters to have a totally different outlook on life. Your whole sense of values should be different. The world thinks of money, of physical and material things. If it is something that will feed your stomach, if it is something that will excite your senses, if it is something that will give you a physical delight, if it is something that will stimulate your desires, then it is something worth while. Those are the values the world appreciates and strives for. God says: "You must have a different sense of values. Your whole ideas of life must be transformed. Your interests in life, your approach to life, how you think about your job, how you feel toward your fellow men, what your hopes, your ambitions, your desires are, everything must be different from the way the world thinks and feels about these things." You are a Christian. As such you do not go to work just to get a pay check; you go to work to serve your fellow men, to use the talents which God has given you to glorify Him, and to serve your brothers and sisters. You do not operate a business just to see how quickly you can make money out of it, how rich you can get. You operate a business because you have some honest ware which is of value to your fellow men. You want to produce the best that you can. You want to give as much work and employment to other men as you can. You are so grateful to God for such opportunities, and so you have a totally different conception of life from the view of the world. You are not a doctor because you get so much for taking out someone's infected appendix. You are not a dentist because you get so much for taking out a tooth. You are in these professions because here you have a noble opportunity to help those of your fellow men who are in pain, who are suffering, and you thrill to the privilege which is yours of doing something that pleases God and that so obviously helps your fellow men.

So, you see, your whole view of life must be different. You are not living for this little day. You are not conceiving of your journey as consisting of so many days, so many weeks, so many years, on this terrestrial sphere. You are thinking of yourself as a child of God who is heading for a heavenly home. So don't put yourself into one class with the world. "Be ye transformed by the renewing of your mind." Your whole attitude toward life, your whole outlook on life, your whole philosophy of life, as we like to say nowadays, must be that of one who is a son or a daughter of God.

GOD PLEADS FOR HUMILITY

But you say: "Now, God, how, specifically, is this to be done?" He says: "My child, listen, I will tell you through Paul, who says: 'I say, through the grace given unto me, to every man that is among you, *not to think of himself more highly than he ought to think, but to think soberly according as God hath dealt to every man the measure of faith.*' I plead with you, My children, behave as My sons and daughters. Be humble."

And, oh, how important that plea is! It always has been and never has ceased to be a very necessary plea. We humans are all inclined to be extremely proud, sensitive. Each of us is inclined to think more of himself than he ought to think. It would take many books to try to tell the story of the havoc which the devil has wrought in the Church of God because of men's pride. It is so easy for people in their pride to get into conflict with one another. Many a Christian congregation has been destroyed, rent asunder, because some members within it were proud in their attitude toward others. It hurts you just to think what the Church of Jesus Christ could be like on this earth were it not for the damage done by human pride—pride on the part of the laity, pride on the part of the clergy, the theologians.

It is so hard for us to be humble, and yet it ought not to be if we remember that we are followers of Jesus. Jesus was not proud. If anybody had a right to be proud, it was He, but He was not. Jesus did not hesitate to take little urchins up on His lap, pat their heads, give them His blessing. Jesus was not too proud to sit down at a table with harlots and publicans. He did not mind being gathered with fishermen in a boat along the banks of the Galilean Sea, with all the smell and the dirt and what not that went with it. He was very humble. He said: "The Son of Man came not to be ministered unto, but to minister." He said: "Let him who would be greatest among you be your servant." Toward the close of His glorious ministry He took one final opportunity to teach a very impressive lesson. He took a basin of water and a towel and got down on the floor and washed the feet of His disciples. You see, there was no pride there. He was very humble. Would God that we might learn that. If you and I can be humble, then we will not be repulsed by each other's faults. We will rather try to help one another. We will all find our place. We will have in our hearts the spirit of forgiveness. We will be so conscious of our common shortcomings, we will not be ready to criticize the shortcomings of others, and thus we will put a cross through the devil's program. He shall not succeed in destroying and disturbing the peace of our

parish by using you or me as his tools and finding our pride
as the avenue through which he operates.

Then our Lord says further: "Now, if you want specific
information as to what to do to heed My plea, I have yet one
thing to say to you. Again I am speaking through the Apostle:
'As we have many members in one body and all members
have not the same office, so we, being many, are one body
in Christ and everyone members one of another.'" Jesus
pleads with you. Be one. Be united. This is His picture: You
have a body. This body is composed of various limbs and
organs. You have your arms, your hands, your legs, your
feet. You have your head, your eyes, your stomach. Each of
these has a certain function to perform. One cannot act for
the other. Each must do its part, and all together they make
a unit—they make you, your body. So God says to you: "My
Church is one body. Jesus is the Head, and you are the members of this body. Each of you has a function to perform, and
your job is to dovetail these functions. Let every one of you
use the talents which I have given him. Now, to do your
job, remember you are all one. You are not working at cross
purposes. You are not working against one another. You are
not each to go off on a tangent, working for yourself, but you
are to co-operate. You are to work together.

"You see, the world does not know how to do that, but you
are My children. You should know how to do it. I have distributed a great variety of gifts, and I want them all used
co-operatively for the upbuilding of My Church. To some
of you I have given the ability to teach. You must teach,
teach young, teach old. To some of you I have given the
ability to bear witness. You know how to approach people.
You know how to walk into a man's office or to go into a

family's home. You know how to talk to them about My love in Christ. So you go out and win people. You bring them in. To some of you I have given a special place in human society to exercise a particular influence. You have a place where you can influence a great many people; so I expect you especially to be the light of the world, the salt of the earth. Use that influence."

This is something very real. Only the other day a Christian businessman who has a very important position and hundreds of people under his guidance told me how comparatively simple it had been to effect a change in the attitude of this whole department, which was under his direction. His predecessor had been a very hard-drinking man. Whenever the department had meetings, it was taken for granted that excessive drinking would be a part of the program. That man died. Then this Christian came into this position. He decided that he was going to do something different. His department was no longer going to be characterized by heavy drinking. So he cut it out of the program. He just did not drink. The result has been almost a transformation of the attitudes of the people who come to their meetings, who serve in that department. They know that the leader has a different set of ideals. So some of you are out there in the world where you have a grand opportunity to influence a great many people.

Some of you have been given a warm personality. You can be the individuals in the family life of our parish who work for finer harmony and better fellowship among the total membership. Some of you know just how to do that. You know how to help this one get acquainted with that one. So that is your business. Some of you have experience in management. Well, here is a parish with a large program to be managed. I could not tell you how many hours of my time have been given since September first just to managing the affairs of the church. Some of you have that ability to give leadership in the organizational life, to see that everything is done in the smoothest way, so that with least effort we get the greatest amount of good.

You are all part of one body. Remember, each of you has a function to perform. Now, live like God's sons and daughters, and perform your function. Some of you can do something extra in the way of giving. The Lord is allowing you to make more money than you need. You are the ones who can give larger sums. You can see to it that the work of the Church can go on unhampered by financial need, more missionaries can be sent out, more teachers can be hired. So, you see, God has something for every one of you to do. Some of you may not be so well, so strong. Perhaps you just spend your days quietly sitting in your home. Well, your heavenly Father has something for you to do. You pray. You have time for meditation. Pray for your church. Pray for God's blessing upon every Christian testimony to the truth. Pray for your minister so that he may preach the Word with power and effectiveness. Pray for the teaching of the little ones in the school and Sunday school. Pray for all your brothers and sisters in the fold. Pray. There is something for each of you to do. Do it.

"I beseech you, brethren, by the mercies of God, do these things." If you will, your Father will be so happy. Your soul will know that peace which cannot be found in any other way, and the Church will stand up in its glory and loveliness in a world which is made sordid and ugly by sin and evil. I beseech you, brethren, heed the plea of God.

A True, Living Church

❖   ❖   ❖

*Having, then, gifts differing according to the grace that is given to us—whether prophecy, let us prophesy according to the proportion of faith; or ministry, let us wait on our ministering; or he that teacheth, on teaching; or he that exhorteth, on exhortation; he that giveth, let him do it with simplicity; he that ruleth, with diligence; he that showeth mercy, with cheerfulness. Let love be without dissimulation. Abhor that which is evil; cleave to that which is good. Be kindly affectioned one to another with brotherly love; in honor preferring one another; not slothful in business; fervent in spirit; serving the Lord; rejoicing in hope; patient in tribulation; continuing instant in prayer; distributing to the necessity of saints; given to hospitality. Bless them which persecute you; bless, and curse not. Rejoice with them that do rejoice, and weep with them that weep. Be of the same mind one toward another. Mind not high things, but condescend to men of low estate. Be not wise in your own conceits.—*ROMANS 12:6-16.

EVERYBODY MUST WORK

Today God would tell us "what we must do to have a live, strong, active Christian congregation." First, He says, *we must all go to work.*

Our Lord has distributed a variety of gifts. To some He has given the gift of prophecy, to others the ability to teach, to others the responsibility to exhort or to cheer, to comfort, and the like. Every member of our congregation has been given some talent which he or she can and should use in the interest of our Lord's kingdom, for the upbuilding of the Church, for the good of the individual members, for the benefit of those who are yet to be won for Christ. No Christian congregation can be alive and achieve what under God it ought achieve to the glory of His name and for the good of human society unless all members put their hand to the task. We are to learn here, as in all other matters of Christian life, from our blessed Lord.

Jesus came into this world to do a specific task. He came to seek and to save that which was lost. Never for a single moment did our Lord permit His eyes to be taken off the goal toward which He was striving. Many temptations were thrown in His way. Many efforts were made to divert Him from His program, but never were they made with success. He gave Himself to that one task, and He did so with a complete devotion, with a holy, untiring, and unrelenting zeal. He pressed on toward the goal. He effected our salvation. This is our comfort and our inspiration.

If we want a Christian congregation to be a living and throbbing group, a power for good in the lives of individuals, in terms of the community, and from the viewpoint of the whole human family, then we as individuals must use those particular talents which we have in application to the work of our God. Some of you have had excellent formal training. Some of you have had very broad experiences in life. All of you have something.

You know, I think, without my making much ado about it, that we do not have that kind of co-operation today.

Perhaps we have an appreciable percentage of our people who are participating in the real work of the church, but there are too many of you who are not participating. You don't have time. You are much too busy with other things. Your interests lie elsewhere, and so you manage somehow to eliminate from your program of active endeavor the real work for which our Lord allows the Church to go on and allows this world yet to stand.

These words of Paul addressed to the Christians at Rome should arouse us: "Having, then, gifts differing according to the grace that is given to us, whether prophecy, let us prophesy according to the proportion of faith; or ministry, let us wait on our ministering; or he that teacheth, on teaching; or he that exhorteth, on exhortation; he that giveth, let him do it with simplicity; he that ruleth, with diligence; he that showeth mercy, with cheerfulness."

The preacher should not act as though he were a martyr. If it is his privilege to preach, he should do so with joy. And the member of the congregation should not feel that he is imposed upon because he has an invitation to do this or to do that. All of us together must do our work in a way which reveals very clearly that our heart is in it and that we rejoice in the privilege which is ours.

EVERY CHRISTIAN SHOULD BE KIND

If we want to be a Christian congregation which has the spirit of Christ in it, then *we must also learn to be kind.* Paul wrote to these Christians at Rome: "Be kindly affectioned one to another with brotherly love."

There is not too much kindness in this world in which we live. As a matter of fact, the world is very cruel. People are inclined to be quite inconsiderate of one another. They are self-centered. Everybody goes out to get what he can for himself. The world thinks that the people who are most successful in this respect are the really wise and the great people in this world. Our Lord had a different attitude. His was one of kindness. He met with all sorts of people from every walk of life, but He met them all with the same spirit. His heart went out to them. It did not make any difference whether they were of high degree or low degree, whether they occupied a position of prestige or whether they belonged to the army of forgotten men. He was kind to the sick and to the hungry and to those who had fallen into great and gross sins. He did not turn away from them or coldly pass them by. He had the gracious word, the helping hand, and the cheerful note of mercy and forgiveness for all. This, now, is to be our attitude toward one another in particular and toward our fellow men in general. God has given to us a variety of things. He gives us earthly things. He gives us life. He gives us education and so on, and all of these things we are to use for the common good of one another in the spirit of genuine kindness.

This kindness is to manifest itself especially also over against those who may not be kind toward us. "Bless them which persecute you; bless, and curse not." Our Lord would have us reward evil with good. You will be like the world if you are unkind and if you have in your heart the spirit of vengeance. If you are determined to pay back in the same coin in which men pay you, then you are not in the spirit of Christ. So if ours is to be a Christian congregation and the spirit of Jesus is to be in our midst, then we must learn kindness from Him. We all make our mistakes. We all say things and do things at one time or another which we ought not to do. Out in the world we must expect that people will try to avenge themselves, but in the Church of Christ our behavior must be different. Whether we be here or whether we be elsewhere, we must try, as the Spirit of God gives us the ability to bear with one another, to have toward one another the attitude of kindness and forgiveness. If someone says something to you which hurts you, or does something which makes you feel bad, then as a follower of Jesus it is for you to respond with the spirit of forgiveness, with love and graciousness. If we can have such a spirit in our congregation, then there will be a mark of distinction which will distinguish the Christian congregation from the world, where vengeance and hatred and selfishness are the prevailing forces.

Further, our Lord says, if we want to have a living Christian congregation, *we must express this kindness also in mutual helpfulness.* He told the Roman Christians that they should be hospitable, distributing to the necessity of the saints. In that day that had particular significance. Christians were often driven out of their homes. They had to flee for their lives because they were Christians. When these Christians rapped at the door of another Christian, in whatsoever community it might have been, our Lord expected them to be received with the spirit of hospitality. Today this problem presents itself in a different way. We do not have persecuted Christians coming to our homes at night asking for food and a night's lodging and protection from the pursuing enemy, but we do have a great many people rapping at our doors from all parts of the world who are crying for our help. In Asia and in Europe there are masses of people who do not know today whom they should turn to. They are hungry. They are naked. They are homeless. Many of them stand all alone. Parents have been lost. Brothers and sisters have become separated from one another, and so they are all alone. They are the people who today are rapping at our doors, seeking admittance to our homes, to our hearts, and waiting for us to extend the helping hand. Inasmuch as we desire to be Christians, whose heart responds to the love of Jesus Christ, we must show this spirit of our Lord by the way in which we reply to those whose appeals reach our ears and our hearts. So the note of selfishness dare not be the dominant note. It must be the note of kindliness, of love, of mutual helpfulness.

EVERY CHRISTIAN SHOULD BE HUMBLE

Further, our Lord says through the Apostle: *"If you want to be a Christian congregation, then you must be humble.* 'Be of the same mind one toward another. Mind not high things, but condescend to men of low estate. Be not wise in your own conceits.' "

The men and women who were in military service had, I think, quite an object lesson in the difference between pride and humility. We all used to read a great deal about the brass hats in the Army and gold braid in the Navy, and people in service had an opportunity to see how pride struts. We find this same spirit very widespread. People are affected by it, and unfortunately too often it finds its way into the church. If we want to have a Christian congregation which is going to do a co-operative job for God, then we must meet one another in the spirit of humility. We cannot have every member in the choir sing the solos. We cannot have everybody be the director of the choir. We cannot have everybody function as an elder in the church, or as the president of the women's society, or as the superintendent of the Sunday school. We must have some who will serve as leaders, and some who will serve as followers. And we must have for all of us the spirit which is ready to make a contribution to the common task. You cannot have a Christian congregation if the individual members will sit around and see if someone is going to slight them. You will have no trouble finding that you have been slighted if you do. You will also discover very quickly that this is not the spirit of Christianity. Our Lord was the sinless Son of God, but He had no hesitancy to become man and be born of the Virgin in the humblest, the most humiliating of circumstances. He was ready to have men spit in His face and slap Him and crown Him with thorns and in the spirit of mockery clothe Him with a purple garment. He was ready to die the most shameful death anyone could die in that day, death on the Cross. He did it all because He loved you. He did it because He was determined to take away your sins. He wanted you to be free from the sense of guilt and from the fear of death. He wanted you to know that by trusting in Him you would be assured of an eternal salvation. He wants you to see from His unfailing love that He would be always at your side and that you can always count on Him as your Friend.

This Lord is the One in whom we must trust for our salvation and after whom we must pattern. He would have us find in Him not only forgiveness for our sins, but also the pathway in which we must walk, the example which we should emulate as we make our way through life. So, as we live with one another, and as we encounter our fellow men whoever they may be and wherever we may find them, ours should be the spirit of humility, the kind of spirit which was in the heart of Jesus.

EVERY CHRISTIAN SHOULD HAVE AN UNDERSTANDING HEART

If we want to be a Christian congregation throbbing with spiritual life and different from the world, which does not know Christ, *then we must also have an understanding heart.* We must be sympathetic toward one another and toward other human beings. We are told: "Rejoice with them that do rejoice, and weep with them that weep. Be of the same mind one toward another." The ministry of Jesus was characterized by His understanding heart. When He saw the lonely leper who pleaded with Him: "Lord, if Thou wilt, Thou canst make me clean," He did not just say to him: "I will, be thou clean." Oh, no! He knew what had gone on in this man's heart. He knew that he had been segregated, exiled from his community. He was a lonely human being whose heart was crying out for the warm hand of someone who loved him and cared for him. So Jesus did not merely speak a word and help him, but He went over and touched him. This was something that nobody else had done for a long, long time.

When great masses of people were gathered around Him as He preached on the mountain side, He did not think only of the message He wanted to convey to them, but He thought of them, their most elementary physical needs. He said: "I cannot let these people go away without food. They haven't had anything to eat for a long time." And so He encouraged His disciples to gather whatever food there was available.

When a poor woman who had fallen into shame and disgrace by her sinful life was brought to Him, our Lord's heart bled for her. Nobody felt the seriousness of her sins more than He did, but He was not thinking about Himself. He was thinking about her, and so His heart went out to her. While others were willing to stone her to death, others who themselves were not spotless and out of whose hearts had come the same kind of lusts and desires as had come out of this woman, Jesus looked up into her face with love and assured her of forgiveness. He started her off on a new path.

This is the thing which is so necessary in our day. We are perplexed by a great many problems, but why have these problems arisen? Largely because there has been no sympathetic understanding in the hearts of some people over against other people. Not so many years ago the people who were the leaders in business had no understanding for the people who worked for them. This applied to so large a degree that a very great rift was created between employers and employees. The situation got so bad that the Government had to enter in and all sorts of laws had to be passed, which then were imposed upon the business community of America. Gradually the employees began to assert their power. They are numerically by far the stronger. When they came into power, they showed just as little regard for their employers as the employers had shown toward them. So today we have this peculiar situation: the Government must pass legislation imposing restraints on the workers. You see, there is so little sympathetic understanding. The one does not try to find out what the problems of the other really are.

We see this in our criticism of people in general. You have heard it said many times, perhaps you have said it, as I have said it: "It is too bad that the poor people who for the first time have been getting more money than they ever had before are the very people who squander it." People who during the days of the war earned amounts of money which were far beyond any amount they expected to earn will probably be the first in the bread line when times change. Their War Bonds and all will be spent because they did not know what to do with the money when they had it. Why do they behave that way? Because they had never been trained to handle surplus funds. If we are sympathetic, we can see why they behave as they do. They have come into the possession of something which they did not know how to use.

You have often heard people express very harsh judgment about the Negroes, their superstitions, their immoralities, their want of cleanliness, haven't you? Perhaps all of us feel somewhat like that about them, but certainly you dare not feel that way and cannot feel that way if you take a sympathetic view of them. How can they be anything but ignorant if nobody ever gave them any schools in which to be trained? How can they be anything but superstitious if the Christians have not ministered to them in a spirit of love and kindness and over past generations tried to bring to them the story of Christ, who is also their Redeemer? How can they know what to do with wash tubs and clean houses when in all the past they have always lived in tumble-down shacks?

So you see, what the world needs is the sympathetic and the understanding heart. Jesus had it. If we want to have a Christian congregation with the emphasis on the word "Christian," not just a congregation, but a Christian congregation, with the spirit of Christ in it, then we must have the sympathetic and understanding heart. We must try to see one another in our respective places in life. When you behave in a certain way at a certain time, that doesn't mean that you are to be condemned right away. Perhaps you are not feeling well that day. Well, then it is our task to try and understand you. We must try to see one another against the background of our daily experiences, our physical condition, the situations prevailing in our home; must try to see what kind of Christian background and training we had. You cannot judge everybody by the same standards. We must try to see one another where we are and be sympathetic. If we have that kind of an understanding in our relation to one another, then the spirit of the Church will be different from the spirit of the unbelieving world. The Church will have a mark of distinction which sets it apart as the Church of Christ.

CHRISTIANS SHOULD BE SINCERE

Beyond all this now, if we want to be a Christian congregation, then *we must be genuine and sincere.* This is the way the Lord put it: "Let love be without dissimulation. Abhor that which is evil; cleave to that which is good." The word *sincerity* does not find too much application in the world of men as we commonly conceive of this world. Statesmen have gloried in their ability to deceive one another. Even at this late date in the history of mankind, statesmen are not yet ready to talk straightforward language. They still try to find phrases and expressions which will hide and conceal the true motives. What they are really after is selfishly to grab something for themselves and their people. They are not honestly trying to find something that will be good for the whole human family. They don't care much what happens to the rest of humanity, just so they and theirs are taken care of. We have abundantly expressed such sentiments in our own country. We probably have people in Grace Church who would condemn American statesmen if that were not their approach. We would condemn our statesmen if they did not prove to be good horse traders. The idea that we are going to have an open heart for the rest of the human family and that we are honestly and generously going to share with them in our cultural, spiritual, economic blessings which the almighty God has poured out over us in such abundance, that is just an idealist's dream. There is no reality about that. That is all long-haired and wild-eyed and does not belong to the actual life of men. "You cannot say that. You must not say it that plainly. You must always act as though you were motivated by high ideals, such as the good-neighbor policy and the respect for the dignity of the human being; but don't carry it too far. Don't turn words and ideas into acts and facts."— That is not sincere. That kind of spirit will not go in the Church of Jesus Christ. If we want to be a Christian Church, we must be genuine. We are so accustomed to insincerity that we almost take it for granted. One person will pass another; he will smile and say "Good morning" to him, and deep down in his heart he will feel bitterness. We say "Thank you" for things we don't appreciate at all. Our lives are shot through with insincerities. Men can behave themselves with all the outward forms of propriety over against ladies and yet in their hearts conceive of a woman with no thought of honor at all. There is so much of the superficial and the false in life.

You cannot have a Christian congregation in which that sort of spirit prevails. If nowhere else in this world, then in the Church of Christ there must be sincerity. If someone has done wrong, then we must honestly say: "That is wrong. You cannot do that. Christians do not behave that way." When we speak to one another, we must not try to make nice words which we do not mean; but we must learn to speak to one another from the heart, honestly and sincerely. "Let love be without dissimulation." As Christians we are not to wear masks and give ourselves a false front, but we are to be honest, forthright, so that we can understand one another, trust one another, work with one another. That is the spirit of Christ and of Christianity.

If we can have that kind of congregation in which everybody works; in which everybody tries to give expression to the spirit of kindness which is in the heart of Jesus; in which we meet one another humbly, in love preferring one another; in which we try to understand one another, then I will assure you that you as individuals will be very happy people. Your lives will be noble and beautiful. And as a Christian congregation we shall be distinguished from the world. The world will not be able to escape the fact that we are people who do behave differently. Ours will be the kind of congregation people will be happy to belong to. There will be something so beautiful and attractive about it that folks from the outside will want to be a part of it. We will really give meaning to the words of our Lord: "Let your light so shine before men that they may see your good works and glorify your Father which is in heaven."

May God in His infinite mercy help us by His Holy Spirit to achieve these wonderful ideals for God, for ourselves, and for the good of our fellow men.

How to Overcome Evil

❖   ❖   ❖

*Recompense to no man evil for evil. Provide things honest in the sight of all men. If it be possible, as much as lieth in you, live peaceably with all men. Dearly beloved, avenge not yourselves, but rather give place unto wrath; for it is written: Vengeance is Mine; I will repay, saith the Lord. Therefore if thine enemy hunger, feed him; if he thirst, give him drink; for in so doing thou shalt heap coals of fire on his head. Be not overcome of evil, but overcome evil with good.—*ROMANS 12:17-21.

EVIL IS REAL

The Epistle for today is designed to teach us how to overcome evil. When we consider this text in somewhat greater detail, we find, first of all, that evil is a very real thing and that we cannot overcome it by merely ignoring the fact that it exists. There are some cults in vogue in our time which try to bring comfort to the human heart by deluding people into believing that there is no such thing as evil. Here, as in many other respects, the Bible again is remarkable because of its realistic facing of facts. The Bible is honest and forthright and frank. It acknowledges the sad and bitter truth that there is evil.

You and I know that we cannot solve the problem of evil

by ignoring its reality, because we know that the Bible is correct in its statement that there is evil. You know this is correct because of the evil that is in yourself. We need but watch the behavior of our own hearts and minds, our own tongues, for a little while, and we shall discover very quickly how much evil there is in this world. When the Apostle speaks of evil in the words of our particular text, however, he is not thinking momentarily of the evil that is within us so much as of the evil which we suffer at the hands of others.

This, too, we know to be a fact. You know it from personal experience. You have been hurt, offended, slandered, maligned, treated with contempt, envied many times in life. You know precisely what that means because of your own everyday experiences. We find this to be true in the individual homes. How beautiful life would be if all of us would refrain from hurting our dear ones! But we don't. We lose our temper. We hurt them. They lose their temper. They hurt us. Even in the home, in the circle of husband and wife, brothers and sisters, parents and children, there are jealousies, attitudes of envy, and the like. Just how much evil there is in this world we can see also from the behavior of class against class, nation against nation, race against race. We have experienced so much in this respect within our own day and generation that one can scarcely believe it to be possible. Human beings can be so unkind, so hard, so cruel, to one another that they even wage wars and ruthlessly plan one another's destruction.

We find evil of this nature manifesting itself even in the church. We must not suppose that we cannot and do not hurt one another because we are a Christian group. No, we do. We are selfish. We are thoughtless. It is so easy for us to speak the unkind word and to do the unkind thing. We can never afford to be careless on this score. I hope that so long as the responsibility of being a pastor will be mine, God will give me enough spiritual insight to get up every day armed with a high-powered rifle, figuratively speaking, looking for the devil, who would try to destroy peace and happiness within the Christian congregation. It has been a rather remarkable thing during the past year to observe the movements of evil trying to disturb, to injure, the work of God as represented in our own parish. Repeated efforts have been made to disturb our people, to undermine their confidence, to raise questions and doubts. Now and then people have come to me, members of our congregation, and they have asked with a good deal of anxiety: "Is it true that you are going to give up the ministry? Is it true that you are going to quit preaching and go into radio work and writing?" Thank God, these things have come from the outside. Our members have been disturbed because they have heard rumors that anonymous letters have been sent to me and all that sort of thing.

It doesn't make any difference where we are, in our homes or in the church, evil is always at work. It was not for nothing God said: "Be sober, be vigilant, because your adversary, the devil, as a roaring lion, walketh about, seeking whom he may devour." The forces of evil are always present. They are always trying to disturb, to undermine, the work of God, to destroy the peaceful and harmonious relationships in a Christian congregation.

OVERCOME EVIL WITH GOOD

What are we to do about it? What can we do to overcome evil? What can a wife do if her husband is mean to her? What should a husband do if his wife is mean to him? What should parents do if their children are mean and unkind to them and hurt them? What should one member in a Christian congregation do if another member in the congregation is mean and unkind to him? What should an employer do if he has an employee who is ugly and unkind? Or what should an employee do who has an employer who is not altogether kind and decent and honest? What should the Russians do now with the German people after the German armies came into their country, devastated vast areas, raped their women, killed their children, and set back their economy for decades and decades? What should we do with the Japanese people after they have destroyed our boys on Iwo Jima and Bataan?

You and I know how our hearts react to the question. If we do what we have an impulse to do, the answer is very simple. Then we will strike back as hard as we can. We will demand an eye for an eye and a tooth for a tooth. We will let them know just how hard we can hit when we hit. Even though we are Christians, we still feel that impulse. The disciples of Jesus felt it. You remember that when Jesus was passing through Samaria and His disciples went ahead to make arrangements for a night's lodging, the Samaritans said: "We don't want Him. Keep Him out of our community." The disciples came back and reported with broken hearts what they had experienced. They said to Jesus, "Why don't You call down fire and brimstone from heaven and destroy these wicked people?" That was their idea. They had the same thought when Jesus was being taken captive. They said, "Lord, shall we smite with the sword?" Peter didn't even wait for the answer. He struck. We are all ready to grit our teeth and show our fangs, as it were, and take revenge. We think that is the way to overcome evil. Use evil to overcome evil. But that is not God's way.

If you really want to learn how to overcome evil, then listen to God. He has an altogether different method. He says: "Recompense to no man evil for evil. . . . Therefore, if thine enemy hunger, feed him; if he thirst, give him drink. . . . Be not overcome of evil, but overcome evil with good." He does not say: "If your mother is hungry, if your employee, your boss, your husband, your wife, your children, are hungry, feed them." No, He says: "If your enemy is hungry, feed him; and if he thirsts, give him to drink." That is the way to overcome evil.

You cannot overcome evil in your home by meeting ugliness with ugliness and unkindness with unkindness. Finally, there is only one way to cope with evil, and that is by love. Yes, it is true, you can restrain evil by force. With the club and with the gun, the police can hold in restraint thieves and murderers and others who would violate the rights of their fellow men. Our nation can hold some weaker nation in restraint with its Army, its Navy, and its bombers. You can restrain evil by force, but you cannot so overcome evil. You still have the evil. So if we want to overcome evil anywhere, we must overcome it by love and by kindness. I can always hold a child in the confirmation class in restraint. Certainly, it should not be difficult for a person my size to handle a thirteen- or a fourteen-year-old if it is merely a question of physically restraining him. But I can never by such methods make a child love his Catechism, his Savior, or work within his heart any desire to learn the things which I am trying to teach. Anyone who anywhere wants to overcome evil must overcome it by love, by kindness.

This applies in your home. If you do not have the happiness in your home which you desire, the answer is not to meet ugliness with ugliness, but to meet unkindness with love. You cannot win in any other way. The same truth applies in the relationship of classes, races, and nations to one another.

It is sad to look out on the world of industry in our country today. We know that when times are bad and jobs are scarce, some businessmen will tend to take advantage of it by paying the lowest possible wages. When times are good and workers are hard to find, some working people immediately come with reprisal and take advantage. They want the highest pay for the least amount of work they can possibly get by with. They think it quite all right to loaf, to steal time, to commit sabotage. You cannot overcome evil that way. You are only hardening people's hearts, dividing them into two camps, and creating a situation in which war will go on and on to the detriment of both sides. We are in a position of power now so that we could take revenge on the Japanese and German people for starting the war. But we will not overcome evil that way. We will only arouse a bitterness which will be perpetuated in the memories of those people, and one day things will erupt again.

So wherever we must deal with evil, we must leave vengeance and punishment to God. He says, "Vengeance is Mine." You do not have to worry that anybody is going to "get by" with evil. Nobody ever yet has succeeded in doing evil with impunity. Yes, you can do evil, but you cannot get out of it what you would like to get for yourself. The only thing you can get is the retribution of God, nothing else. Our job is not to see how we can square things off with the other fellow, how we can pay him back. Our job is to overcome evil with good.

DIVINE EXAMPLE

Mark well, God has not only told us how to overcome evil. No, He has shown us how it should be done. When man fell into sin, this was a slap in the face of God. God had given everything to man. He had put him into an environment which met his every need and provided him with perfect happiness. Man responded with ingratitude. One would have imagined that under the circumstances God would have struck back, that God would have ended it right then and there, but He didn't. It is true, He disciplined man. He took from him the enjoyment of Paradise, but He met him in the spirit of love. He gave him the promise of a Savior who was to come: "I will put enmity between thee and the woman, and between thy seed and her Seed. It shall bruise thy head, and thou shalt bruise His heel." God met sin and evil with the answer of love.

Throughout the Old Testament period, God returned again and again with the promise of love. He assured His people: "A Savior is going to come. I love you. I am going to redeem you. Trust in this Messiah."—God kept His promise. He sent Jesus. It was a tremendous price. Jesus, the Son of God, became man. He did not allow man to go to his doom under the curse of sin, but He reached down for him. He came for you. He suffered the infinite torments of hell. He died on the accursed tree. Every shame, disgrace, and humiliation that could be heaped upon Him He bore for you.

God does not only *say*, "Overcome evil with good," no, that is the way God *does* it. That is how He overcame evil for you. If you believe in Jesus, then you know what a wonderful blessing this is. Then you know how sweet it is to have in your heart this heavenly peace, this divine assurance: "My God loves me. Evil has been overcome for me by the love of my Redeemer."

OVERCOME EVIL THROUGH CHRIST

If you have never yet accepted Christ, then I would certainly plead with you to do so. You cannot overcome the evil in your own heart and the curse of sin in your own life without this love of God. It is the only answer to your problem. Take this Christ. Say to Him: "You are my Lord. I trust in You." When you speak that word with faith, then you know that evil has been overcome by good.

By this same love, God also overcomes the evil that is in your heart and that leads you to the doing of evil things. God is not satisfied merely to pay your debts. God wants to improve your life, ennoble your character, give you the capacity to live as His children should live. How does He do it? By beating you into proper behavior, into forms of conduct that are pleasing to Him? Oh, no!

Can you imagine a hollow curved tube of glass both ends of which are open? If it is what we call an "empty" tube, then you know that it is filled with air. Now, if you run water into one end of the tube, it drives the air out the other end. Again, if you blow air into the one end, it will displace the water. That is a very crude picture of what God does for you. You have sin in your heart, so God brings His love into your heart. As His love comes into your heart, sin is pushed out of the heart. When you give place to sin in your heart, you push the love of God out; and when you give place to the love of God, you push sin out.

So God by love would overcome sin in your life; not by force, not by threats, not by fear—by love. Not even God can overcome evil in your own heart except by love. That is the great truth which our Lord would teach us. By love He has overcome evil for us so that we through Christ can have peace and forgiveness. By His love He would replace evil in our hearts so that we can live lives of grateful response to the love which He has shown us. And by love would He have us overcome the evil which we encounter in our relationships with one another and with all our fellow men around the globe.

"Be not overcome of evil, but overcome evil with good." May God help you in this for Jesus' sake. Amen.

Are You Winning the Race of Life?

❖ ❖ ❖

Know ye not that they which run in a race run all, but one receiveth the prize? So run that ye may obtain. And every man that striveth for the mastery is temperate in all things. Now, they do it to obtain a corruptible crown; but we, an incorruptible. I therefore so run, not as uncertainly; so fight I, not as one that beateth the air. But I keep under my body and bring it into subjection; lest that, by any means, when I have preached to others, I myself should be a castaway. Moreover, brethren, I would not that ye should be ignorant how that all our fathers were under the cloud and all passed through the sea; and were all baptized unto Moses in the cloud and in the sea; and did all eat the same spiritual meat; and did all drink the same spiritual drink; for they drank of that spiritual Rock that followed them; and that Rock was Christ. But with many of them God was not well pleased: for they were overthrown in the wilderness.—I CORINTHIANS 9:24-10:5.

WANT OF MORAL ENERGY

If Paul the Apostle were an American citizen, I feel rather sure he would want to live in Chicagoland or in some other comparable metropolitan area throbbing with life and activity. Paul was a very dynamic individual, filled with an abundance of spiritual energy. How true that is we can see from the words of the Epistle for today.

Paul was disturbed because the Christians in the congregation at Corinth did not manifest a similar kind of spiritual energy and moral activity. Paul had preached the Gospel to them. He had been able to say: "When I was among you, I professed to know nothing save Christ and Him Crucified." He had told them the beautiful story of how God had redeemed them through Jesus. He had taken them by the hand and led them into the pathways of godliness. He had planted their feet, as it were, on the pathway of life, on which now they were to run. But they were not doing so well. They were fighting among themselves. The congregation was torn into striving factions. They were not very careful about their general conduct. When they got together, they ate immoderately, and they got drunk. All of this was very horrifying to the Apostle. They also connived at some forms of unchastity which were practiced by their members. Paul's heart was trembling for them; so he wrote them to stir them up, to arouse their consciences, to awaken them to the requirements of real Christian living.

What Paul wrote to the Corinthian Christians at that time has its immediate and direct application to us. It raises a very important question for each one of us. It is as though the Apostle were pointing his finger directly at you and saying to you: "How is it with you? Are you winning the race of life?"

Paul was born and reared in the city of Tarsus. He had gained certain childhood impressions which he never forgot. Tarsus was a great city. It had its own university, its own amphitheater. Just as the American boy knows his baseball players and knows which teams are leading the league, so Paul knew the racers and the boxers and other athletes who participated in the contests in his own home town. When Paul wanted to make some moral or spiritual truth clear, he often took his pictures and illustrations from these childhood memories, from the things which he had seen when he was out at the amphitheater and watched the races, the boxing matches, and other contests. Just as we borrow many expressions from America's favorite sport, baseball, so Paul borrowed his expressions and illustrations from the popular sports of his time and his own city, Tarsus. We say of a man who was successful, "He made a home run," or "He got a hit." We say of somebody who failed, "He struck out." These are common expressions in our everyday life, and when we use them, we immediately know everybody in our country understands what we mean.

Since in Paul's day races and athletic contests were very popular, Paul spoke in terms of these, that his people might understand. He said: "Are you winning the race of life? How are you doing?" He had taught them great truths. He had instructed them in the moral requirements of Christian living. He had pointed out for them the goal for which they should strive. He had given them the way that led to the goal. Now, how were they doing? Were they winning the race of life, or were they losing?

HOW ARE YOU DOING?

This question, which Paul addressed to the Christians in Corinth, is addressed to every son and daughter of God. You as a Christian have a race to run. You have a goal toward which you must be striving. There is something out there you want to achieve. You want to win. You have learned about Jesus. You know how God expressed His love for you when He sent that Redeemer. Now, you want to learn all you can about this Christ. You want to discover ever more fully how to apply the love of God in Jesus to yourself, to every need and every aspect of your life. You are eager that the love of Jesus should become a burning fire within you and a mighty impelling force which will give you the strength and the inspiration for living an ever more beautiful life. You have the pattern of Christ's character and life. You want to be as Jesus was. You want to think as He thought. You want to speak as He spoke. You want to act as He acted. You want your life to be expressive of the warm love and the forgiving and understanding heart. You are aware of the weaknesses that are in you. You know your temper, how dangerous your tongue can be, how easily lusts can arise within you, how often you can suspect your fellow men of evil motives. You know how easy it is to forget the spiritual and to give yourself wholly to the pursuit of the temporal and the material. You are familiar with all of this, but that isn't what you want to do. You want to do things in God's way. You want to rise above these weaknesses. You want to overcome them and to develop into an ever fuller and wiser and more mature son or daughter of God. So there is a goal out there toward which you want to strive. How are you doing? Are you making headway in this race, or are you falling by the wayside?

As a follower of Jesus you also have a race to run with reference to social welfare in general. You know that you are not alone in this world. You are living in a world of men. You are living in a world of men so many of whom are unhappy. They do not know God. They know nothing about Jesus, whom He sent to love them, to die for them, to redeem them, to save them from their sins, to give them a happy, easy conscience, to fill their souls with a peace which comes from heaven and which surpasses anything the human tongue can express or the human mind can encompass. They know nothing about all of that. So many of them are desperate.

They are looking for something that will make them happy, but they do not know where to find it. They are in revolt against God and in conflict with one another. Too many, in a spirit of desperation, throw their lives away. They try to forget the realities of life by overeating, by overdrinking, by dissipating, giving themselves to all sorts of lusts and sins. You see life in all its naked tragedy. You know how nations live in mortal fear of one another and wonder which has the deadliest weapons in its armory. Now, it is for you as a Christian to help these poor humans, to go out and win them one by one, to tell them about the love of God in Christ, so that they can have the same kind of peace you have, to wrest them free from the grip of sin, to take them by the hand and lead them with you in the pathways of doing things that are expressive of love and kindness, that take away fear and suspicion and put in their place trust and confidence. These are the things you and I are to do as Christians. This is the race we are to run. How are you doing? Are you winning the race? Or are you not?

I wish we could say with complete assurance that every member of Grace Church were winning the race, but I am afraid we are in the same position in which Paul was when he addressed himself to the Christians at Corinth. Too many of our folks do not understand the seriousness of Christian living, the importance of the spiritual side of life, the really precious value of an immortal soul. They give good care to their bodies. Many at least try to improve their minds. But too many apparently do not quite understand what the needs of their souls are.

TRAINING REQUIRED

Paul wanted the Christians at Corinth to realize that winning the race of life was not an easy matter. He said: "If you want to win that race, you have to stay in trim. You have to keep yourselves in good form." Paul knew that the athletes who wanted to participate in the athletic contests of the Greek world had to swear an oath that during the ten months preceding the contest in which they were going to participate they would put themselves into severe training. It was as though we today would demand of a boy who wanted to play on the football team to swear an oath that he would get himself ready for the contest by not smoking or drinking for ten months before that contest.

Think of it. These Greek athletes were only going to participate in an athletic contest. If they would win, what would they get for it? Probably a crown woven out of parsley greens or olive leaves. It was not worth getting except for the glory, and yet that was the most coveted prize on the part of the young and the athletic in the whole Greco-Roman world.

"Now," says Paul, "you are Christians. You have a race to run. You cannot expect to win, you cannot reach the coveted goal and prize, unless you go into training. You have to get ready for this. You have to keep yourselves in good form; otherwise you are going to fall by the wayside."

They knew what he meant. They had to eat wholesome food, the food which God provided, the Bread of Life, the divine Word. Not a few of our folks must be of the opinion that the divine Word is not too important. Some come very, very seldom into God's house. I think it would not be difficult to find a number of our members who have not been in God's house for months. Probably, if you would investigate, you would discover that they had not been reading their Bible either. If you went far enough in your investigations, you would no doubt find that they are not very ardent and zealous in their prayers. All of these things hang together, and one usually brings on the other. It is all a part of a general picture. They will also be unfaithful in the use of God's Holy Supper.

But how can you be strong if you do not eat the food which God has given to nourish your soul? So when Paul points the finger at you and says: "You cannot win the race of life unless you keep yourself in trim," he is encouraging you to use this food to nourish your soul, to strengthen yourself, to give the Spirit of God an opportunity to enable you to run more successfully.

Training requires more than merely eating good, wholesome food. It also calls for some stiff exercises. You cannot run the race unless you run. You cannot learn to run unless you try it. You have to exercise yourself. So it is in the matter of Christian living.

TRY

You and I are not going to be successful in living our Christian faith and in carrying on the work of God for the good of human society unless we try to do so. We must put our hand to the task. It is something at which you must be constantly practicing. You must try, try, and try again. The simplest entertainer, the juggler, the dancer, the athletic performer, whoever he may be, must have infinite patience. He must try, try, and try again before he can do successfully and effectively what he wants to do for the entertainment and the delight of his fellow men. It is not otherwise with us. As Christians we have our task, our assignment.

So often folks think that to be a Christian is a very simple thing. Nobody can be a Christian, become a member of the Church, and then think all is well. Oh, no! You still have the race of life to run, and you are not going to run it successfully unless you try, get out and exercise, do your daily stint. You must stay with it. Tell me, how is it with you? Are you winning the race of life? Are you exercising yourself in prayer, in the understanding of the truths of God, in the winning of men's souls, in the daily application of the law of love to all parts of life and all your social relationships? Just how is it? Are you winning?

YOU CAN FAIL

Paul wanted the Christians at Corinth to know that this was a very serious business. He wanted them to know that it is possible to fall by the wayside so completely that they miss the goal entirely. He reminded them of the experiences of the Israelites. When the Israelites came out of Egypt to go to the Land of Promise, where milk and honey flowed and where the great promises of God were to find their most glorious fulfillment, they had everything they needed to win success. God had told them about the coming Messiah. He had given them a great and courageous leader, Moses, one of the most memorable names in all history. They had all this. God protected them. He saved them from the hands of Pharaoh, brought them through the Red Sea, and started them on the journey to the Holy Land. But they did not take it very seriously. They made a golden calf for themselves and danced about it. They became like others. They were greedy. When God gave them manna and said: "Take enough for each day. Don't try to lay by a surplus," they were not satisfied. Despite everything God had done for them, they did not trust Him. They tried greedily to get more than they thought God wanted them to have. They yielded to their carnal lusts. The whole thing was such a shameful performance that God allowed thousands of them to die in the desert. They never did see the Promised Land.

So Paul said to the Corinthians: "This is a serious business. Are you winning the race, or are you falling by the wayside?

Remember, you can fall by the wayside and never get to the goal. That is what happened to thousands out there in the desert. They never saw the Land of Promise."

Paul said in effect: "I am acutely aware of this myself. I have the same problem. Here I am fighting. What do you think I am doing, merely beating the air? No, when I box, I want to score a hit. But I am having a terrible time. I have to keep my body under so that while I am preaching to you, I myself do not become a castaway. I have to work at this. I have to fight, or otherwise I, too, will fall by the wayside."

And so it is. This running of life's race is a serious thing. Many who have started to come up in the great spiritual contest have given up. They have fallen by the wayside. They have lost sight of the goal. It can happen to you and to me. So it is a great and important question which is propounded for us today by the Epistle for Septuagesima Sunday. The question is this: "Are you winning the race of life?"

God's Grace Is Sufficient

❖   ❖   ❖

For ye suffer fools gladly, seeing ye yourselves are wise. For ye suffer if a man bring you into bondage, if a man devour you, if a man take of you, if a man exalt himself, if a man smite you on the face. I speak as concerning reproach, as though we had been weak. Howbeit whereinsoever any is bold (I speak foolishly), I am bold also. Are they Hebrews? So am I. Are they Israelites? So am I. Are they the seed of Abraham? So am I. Are they ministers of Christ? (I speak as a fool) I am more; in labors more abundant, in stripes above measure, in prisons more frequent, in deaths oft. Of the Jews five times received I forty stripes save one. Thrice was I beaten with rods, once was I stoned, thrice I suffered shipwreck, a night and a day I have been in the deep; in journeyings often, in perils of waters, in perils of robbers, in perils by mine own countrymen, in perils by the heathen, in perils in the city, in perils in the wilderness, in perils in the sea, in perils among false brethren; in weariness and painfulness, in watchings often, in hunger and thirst, in fastings often, in cold and nakedness. Beside those things that are without, that which cometh upon me daily, the care of all the churches. Who is weak, and I am not weak? Who is offended, and I burn not? If I must needs glory, I will glory of the things which concern mine infirmities. The God and Father of our Lord Jesus Christ, which is blessed forevermore, knoweth that I lie not. In Damascus the governor under Aretas the king kept the city of the Damascenes with a garrison, desirous to apprehend me. And through a window in a basket was I let down by the wall and escaped his hands. It is not expedient for me doubtless to glory. I will come to visions and revelations of the Lord. I knew a man in Christ above fourteen years ago (whether in the body, I cannot tell; or whether out of the body, I cannot tell; God knoweth), such an one caught up to the third heaven. And I knew such a man (whether in the body or out of the body, I cannot tell; God knoweth), how that he was caught up into Paradise and heard unspeakable words, which it is not lawful for a man to utter. Of such an one will I glory; yet of myself I will not glory but in mine infirmities. For though I would desire to glory, I shall not be a fool; for I will say the truth; but now I forbear, lest any man should think of me above that which he seeth me to be or that he heareth of me. And lest I should be exalted above measure through the abundance of the revelations, there was given to me a thorn in the flesh, the messenger of Satan to buffet me, lest I should be exalted above measure. For this thing I besought the Lord thrice that it might depart from me. And He said unto me: My grace is sufficient for thee, for My strength is made perfect in weakness. Most gladly therefore will I rather glory in my infirmities, that the power of Christ may rest upon me.—II Corinthians 11:19-12:9.

DIFFICULTIES

The Christian ministry, when properly attended to, is not always as easy as it seems to be. Paul the Apostle found that out very quickly. He had great ambitions, wonderful dreams, for the upbuilding and extending of Christ's kingdom here on earth. He was determined to put into this task every ounce of strength and energy that God had given. He labored with might and main. It was not long, however, before he discovered that where he labored to build up the Kingdom of God, his enemies worked with equal fervor to tear it down and destroy it.

He discovered quickly, too, that such simple matters as truth and honesty and justice did not bother them very much. They were not asking whether the things they did were right or wrong. They were only concerned about reaching their objectives. They were not going to let the Apostle carry on his work. So one of the easy ways, at least so they thought, to undermine all his efforts, was to slander, defame, and malign him wherever they had opportunity of doing so. So they said: "This man Paul is not a legitimate representative of the Christian religion. He was not one of the Lord's Apostles. He does not come to us from the mother church at Jerusalem. He is not properly authenticated." They said: "The things he teaches are not true. He is deceiving you folks when he tells you that you can get forgiveness by merely accepting Jesus as your Savior. He is lying to you. You must be circumcised to be real covenant members in the Church of God." And so on and so on. They represented Paul as one of those cheap individuals who impose on the gullible masses for the purpose of getting some money out of them. That was one of the reasons why Paul was so very careful from whom he accepted money. He did not want to be supported by most of the congregations whom he served lest people would say that he was preaching only for what he got.

PAUL'S EXPERIENCE WITH GOD'S GRACE

Paul wrote a Letter to the Corinthian Christians. He said in effect: "You have been told all manner of things about me. It is high time I tell you a few things." He then went on to give them his spiritual pedigree, as it were. He told them how he had come into Christian knowledge and understanding. He told them of the wonderful and exceptional spiritual experiences which God in His mercy had given to him. He told about all the work he had been allowed to do for God. Without a blush of shame he said in substance: "I worked more than they all. If anybody has a right to boast, I have." He told them about all the things he had endured in the way of imprisonment and other types of suffering.

When Paul got through with his recital of all these things, it was almost as though he became frightened. He was not trying to sell himself to these people. That was not what he was concerned about. He certainly did not want them to think more of him than they ought to think. He only wanted to be received as an ambassador of Jesus Christ, and he wanted them to believe the message which he preached to them. "But," he said in his own way, "now that you have heard all my boasting, I don't want you to think that God has allowed me to become so inflated and so concerned with my own ego that I am walking in the clouds. No, God saw to it that I would keep my feet on the ground and that I would stay properly humble. He allowed an affliction to come upon me. He gave me a thorn in the flesh." He continued: "This is a terrible thing, and I would like to be rid of it. It hinders me. It hampers me. I have asked God three different times to relieve me of this cross, but He would not do it. He said to me: 'My grace is sufficient for thee, for My strength is made perfect in weakness.'"

GRACE FOUND

Paul knew before this how wonderful the grace of God was in application to his spiritual needs. Paul had grown up in a Jewish home. He had been given the finest kind of Jewish instruction. His ambitious father had sent him to Jerusalem, where he had sat at the feet of Gamaliel, the outstanding teacher in Jerusalem in that day. Paul had been told that the way to get right with God was to do the things that God demanded in the Law. Paul tried that method. He was a serious-minded young man. He was not frivolous. He took his religion seriously. He tried. He tried desperately. But he never reached the point of perfection. He wanted very much to be good. Very much he wanted to be able to say to God, "Now I have done all You ask." But he never got there. God demanded that he should live a perfect and a holy life, and Paul could not make the grade. No matter how he tried, he always fell short. The result was that he never did get real joy for his heart. He never did receive sweet peace for his soul. The Law was always telling him: "Paul, things are not right. You have not done what you should have done. You are always falling short." He said, "I died under the Law." The Law condemned him. He could not get to God. He could not look God in the eye that way. He found no real peace.

Inasmuch as he took his spiritual life seriously and recognized his sins and his shortcomings for what they were, it naturally disturbed his soul no end to know that this problem had not been taken care of. But then one day God came to him—Jesus, the resurrected, the living Lord, the very One whom Paul had been opposing and fighting as a loyal son of Judaism. The Spirit of God came into Paul's heart and changed it. He opened his eyes so that when Paul looked at Jesus, he could say: "This is my Savior. This is the One who died for me. I do not have to work out my own salvation. God gives it to me in His grace and in His love. He makes me a free present of it." Then Paul took it. Paul believed, and for the first time he knew what it meant to be right with God, to have all his sins taken away, to be able to look up to God and to call Him Father. There was no further uncertainty in his heart, and from that moment on Paul was sure of one thing: "We conclude, therefore, that a man is saved not by the deeds of the Law, but by grace, through faith in Jesus Christ." Oh, the sweetness of the grace of God! Of all the things that had come to him in life, nothing had ever been like this grace of God. That brought him inner quiet. It put his heart at rest. Now the voice of his active conscience was quiet and still at last because God in His grace had forgiven his sins.

GRACE FOR YOU

This grace Paul knew, and this grace God would have you know. Here I stand, a sinner, and I look out upon a congregation of sinners, all my fellow sinners. We all come short of the glory wherewith we could stand before God, and God offers us His grace in Jesus, who suffered for us and who died for us. Jesus offers you, God offers you, His grace. All your sins are taken away, and you should not go through life bowed down. You should not go through life with your heart in a constant state of ferment. God does not want your soul to be torn. He does not want you to be beaten and cudgeled by the voice of conscience, which says: "You have done wrong; you have done wrong." He wants you to be happy. He wants peace, peace from heaven, to flood your soul so that you are a lighthearted, happy son or daughter of God. Now, mind you, that applies to every one of you. Certainly, you do not all have the same problems. Some of you may have a more grievous problem this morning than someone else. Yesterday your problem may not have been so grievous. Probably it was somebody else who then had the grievous problem. Tomorrow it may no longer be you, it may be somebody else again who has this heavy thing weighing on his heart.

The other day I was sitting with a poor man, not poor in this world's goods. No, he was abundantly supplied with this world's goods, but poor in things spiritual. He was all atremble. He had been drunk for a month. Doctors and nurses had tried to get him back to some semblance of being a man. Finally the doctor had said to him: "You don't need me. I can't do anything for you. Don't you know some minister, some priest, to whom you could turn?" And so it was that he called me. And when, even in his weakened state, we began to speak about the situation in which he found himself, he finally told of his needs. What was it, money? No, he had plenty of money. What was it that bothered him? It was sin. Sin was ruining the happiness of his soul. He was trying to get away from that relentlessly haunting, pursuing voice inside of him, which said, "You are a sinner." He did not know how to face the accusation.

I do not know what is going on in your soul this morning. I know that you are a sinner like me, and I know that God's free gift of grace is here for you. Take it. Don't let sin ruin your life. Don't deny yourself what God in His grace and goodness wants to give you free. Take it. Just say to Him: "God, I am sorry I am a sinner. I do believe that Jesus died for me." And then the love and the mercy of God will come into your soul, and you will know what it means to have heavenly peace and to be a child of God.

This wonderful story of God's grace and mercy has such peculiar significance for us today because this is the sixteenth anniversary of our church dedication. If it were not for the story of God's grace, there would be no meaning in the dedication of this church. The only reason why this is a happy day for us and why this is a significant building for us and why the work we do here is so glorious to us is that it all deals with the grace of God. Sunday after Sunday we have the privilege of telling the story of how God loves poor sinners. We can tell it to the little ones in the Primary Department and the kindergarten, the school and the Sunday school. We can tell it in the confirmation classes and to the adults. That is a story we can tell to our fellow men in various walks of life. That is why this is such a happy day. God in His mercy has allowed us to carry on His work. He has preserved unto us the wonderful story of His love in Christ. He has allowed us to share this story with our fellow men through the preaching of the Word and through the administration of the Holy Sacraments. That is what gives significance to Grace Church, that and nothing else.

GOD IN GRACE WORKS THROUGH US

Well, Paul, who had learned from personal experience how sweet the grace of God was when applied to his spiritual needs, now was assured by the Spirit of God that he should not worry about the success of his professional life. He should not allow the fact that he had a thorn in the flesh to disturb him. The Lord said to him: "My grace is sufficient for thee, for My strength is made perfect in weakness." He said, as it were: "You just go, Paul, and you keep that thorn in the flesh. What I want to achieve through you I am not going to achieve because you are strong, because you have extra powers of enterprise, but I am going to use you, an afflicted human being, to accomplish My purposes. Men shall know wherever Paul goes, God is doing this thing. This despised little Jew cannot do it, but the Spirit of God working through him can do it.—My grace is sufficient for thee, for My strength is made perfect in weakness."

When Paul heard that assurance, he did not know how true it was going to be. All he could do was to believe it, and he did believe it. Believing, he acted upon it. He went from one assignment to an ever greater assignment, from one big city to an ever bigger city. He did not say: "Oh, that place is too big. I had better not go there." No, he looked at the big places, the hard places, where the masses of people were, and Paul went where the people were. He preached. He could say to these Corinthians: "When I was among you, I professed to know nothing save Jesus Christ and Him Crucified." He did not try to be wise. He did not try to put himself on a level with the Greek philosophers. He only came to be a witness. You have heard the catalog of his experiences as related in the Epistle for today. Few human beings could have endured such suffering, but God kept Paul alive, saw him through all his difficulties, and used them. And by the testimony of this man the Church of Jesus Christ was established, and in great cities, cities which to this day still are great, he built the Church—in Thessalonica, Philippi, Ephesus, Berea, Corinth. Finally he went all the way to Rome, the capital city of the world. "My grace is sufficient for thee, for My strength is made perfect in weakness." It was Christ's work, and Christ deigned to use a weak human being to accomplish His great task. The Lord never failed him.

THANKS BE TO GOD

Today we want to say with gratitude to Almighty God that He has not failed us either. Oh, I wish we could say that we had done more than we have done, that we had achieved greater victories, but the fact still remains—God has used us weak human beings to accomplish His purposes. Here we are. We all have our limitations, that is true. The full-time servants of the congregation all have their limitations, physical limitations, intellectual limitations, limitations of devotion and consecration. And here are you, the army marching under the banner of Christ, and you all have your limitations. Some of you probably would like to do more work for the Kingdom of Christ, but you cannot. Maybe your heart is bad, and you have to rest. Perhaps you have some other physical limitation because of which you can only do so much and no more. Perhaps you are limited in the appreciation of eternal things, limited in your love and devotion to Christ. Some of you have a burning love for the Savior. You say: "I am going to do something for my Lord. I must do something for the upbuilding of Christ's kingdom." Some of you have not progressed to that point yet. Everything else in life is more important. You cannot find time to do anything for the Lord. You are limited in your understanding.

And yet, with all our weaknesses, all of our imperfection, God has been ready to work through us here in order to do something for the upbuilding of His kingdom. During these sixteen years in which we have been housed in this beautiful temple of God we have been allowed to win souls for Christ. Many of you who are here this morning heard the Gospel of Jesus Christ for the first time within the environment of these walls. The other day a gentleman was passing through Chicago. He called me up. I was very happy to hear his voice. He said, "Do you remember me?" I said, "Very well." He came to me one night as an atheist. He was ready to commit suicide. He had been gambling and drinking. His home was falling apart. He needed help. He said: "Do you remember what you said when you were instructing me? You one time told me that if in all your ministry you could bring just one soul to Christ, then your life would have been well spent. I am telling you that you have that to your credit. Here is one soul you have brought to Christ." Well, that is only one. Some of you have brought souls to Christ. Some have moved to other cities. Some of them have already gone on to glory. Yes, God has used us to help others as He used Paul. We have been allowed to teach His Word to little children, many of them. Their number has been growing every passing year. Almost on every Sunday of the year you can be sure that almost one half of the boys and girls in our Sunday school come from homes not affiliated with our church. Think of that! We have the privilege of telling the story of Jesus to boys and girls coming from homes whose fathers and mothers may not have any understanding of it. Not all of these boys and girls will become affiliated with our congregation, but if we have led them to Jesus, we have added more souls to His kingdom.

We have been allowed to preach His Word and to teach it with blessing to our own people. You can read almost any kind of current literature nowadays or look at almost any kind of book, and you encounter some sad voice which says: "Human beings are held in the grip of tensions. They are trying to escape from something. Some of them become neurotics, some of them become alcoholics, some of them commit suicide, because the world is crazy and the human beings are being made crazy by the very environment in which they live." Read almost anything nowadays, and you get the story. The other day I was reading a book dealing with the challenge of present-day culture. The writer was looking at life from the psychologist's point of view. He was enumerating all of these problems. He said: "These problems are bobbing up so often that the psychologists cannot begin to keep up with them." Well, what then? Is there nothing left? Must men be driven to desperation and hopelessness? No, thank God, there is an answer! "Earth has no sorrow that Heaven cannot heal." There is a great God. And I hope we all appreciate the fact that it is a miracle of divine grace when a body of Christians constituting a small village can be preserved by the mercies of God from the beatings and the storms of life, as you have been preserved. We have been held together in these times of strife and of conflict, of love-lessness and hopelessness, we have been held together as a happy family of God's children. God has worked that way through us with all of our weaknesses so that His strength might be made perfect in weakness. What we never could have done for ourselves He in His love has done for us and desires to do for us in the future.

HOPE FOR TOMORROW

Well, that ought to make us happy on the occasion of the sixteenth anniversary of our church dedication and cause us to thank God with all our hearts. But even that is not all. We still have the opportunity to look forward. Here we are in a great world. It presents many problems. Men are trying so frantically to solve these problems. You and I are weak and helpless. We do not know what to do. God says: "Come, I am going to use you in order to accomplish My purposes." Thus you know that we can go on preaching and teaching this Word and that you and I are going to grow spiritually. The fires of love in Christ are going to burn brighter and brighter. Some of you who are cold and indifferent, who can-not find any time for Jesus Christ and His work, you will find time. You, too, will grow. You will learn how with love and devotion to give yourselves to the service of your Lord. You will discover how to distinguish between that which is passing and that which is eternal. God in His mercy will show you. You will learn how to stand up against the things of life, how to resist temptations when they come, how to tear yourselves free from the bonds and chains of sin and take your place by the side of God to live for that which is right. We have God's assurance for it that our work is not going to be in vain. As we tell that story to the little ones, they are going to grow up and develop into men and women who in this world of unbelief and sorrow and sin will take their place with God. As you go into the shop and salesroom, you can help others find out about sin and grace. You will be bringing them in. Thus, one by one, we shall be able to help human beings find peace with God. It will be our privilege, as it was the privilege of Paul the Apostle, to make a contribution to the greater well-being and happiness of human society. All this because the grace of God is sufficient. As we contemplate this, we look forward with joy and hope to tomorrow and the next day, and our hearts overflow with the gratitude which says, "*Soli Deo Gloria,*" to God alone be glory.

The Greatest of These Is Love

❖   ❖   ❖

Though I speak with the tongues of men and of angels and have not charity, I am become as sounding brass or a tinkling cymbal. And though I have the gift of prophecy and understand all mysteries and all knowledge; and though I have all faith, so that I could remove mountains, and have not charity, I am nothing. And though I bestow all my goods to feed the poor, and though I give my body to be burned, and have not charity, it profiteth me nothing. Charity suffereth long and is kind; charity envieth not; charity vaunteth not itself, is not puffed up, doth not behave itself unseemly, seeketh not her own, is not easily provoked, thinketh no evil; rejoiceth not in iniquity, but rejoiceth in the truth; beareth all things, believeth all things, hopeth all things, endureth all things. Charity never faileth. But whether there be prophecies, they shall fail; whether there be tongues, they shall cease; whether there be knowledge, it shall vanish away. For we know in part, and we prophesy in part. But when that which is perfect is come, then that which is in part shall be done away. When I was a child, I spake as a child, I understood as a child, I thought as a child; but when I became a man, I put away childish things. For now we see through a glass, darkly; but then face to face. Now I know in part; but then shall I know even as also I am known. And now abideth faith, hope, charity, these three; but the greatest of these is charity.—I Corinthians *13:1-13.*

The Lenten season is upon us. God willing, we shall again have the joy and spiritual privilege of reflecting particularly upon the infinite love and mercy which God showed us when He sent Jesus into this world to be our Redeemer from sin. This is, always has been, and always will be, the world's most wonderful story.

GOD KNOWS YOUR HELPLESSNESS

It certainly must do something to your heart when you become conscious of the fact that God knows all about you. God is your Father. He looks into your life. He looks into your heart. He sees all your needs. His mercy and grace go out to you because He observes you as a helpless child of His finding itself in the grip of sin. When God looks at you in the power of sin, He sees you as a piece of putty which is being molded by the powers of evil as they would mold you. God sees you in all the misery and in all the heartache that comes out of sin. God observes how you allow yourself to be deceived and how you deceive yourself. You think, and you let the powers of evil get you to think again and again, that your joy consists in wrongdoing. God knows that you are being lied to time without number, and that again and again you follow the lie. God knows what a curse sin is in your life.

He knows how true that is not only for this world, where it causes you all of your heartaches, all of your anguish and agony of soul, where it causes you to be haunted and dogged and tormented by an active, guilty, accusing conscience. He knows that this curse abides also in eternity. Sin means separation from Him. Sin means being forever shut out in darkness where there is weeping and gnashing of teeth. But God does not want you to be haunted. God does not want you to hit your head against a stone wall and to destroy yourself. God wants you to have peace. He wants the light of joy to flood your soul. He wants you to be able to greet each newly dawning day with hope and to come to the close of every busy working day with joy, with comfort in your heart, with a quiet, calm assurance that all is well between you and your heavenly Father. God wants you to be utterly without fear as to the eternity which lies ahead. He does not want you to reckon with the terrors of hell, but He wants you to revel in the anticipation of heaven's unspeakable joys and eternal delights.

GOD PROVIDES HELP

Because God knows what your problem is, and because God in His love wants you to meet that problem and be freed from its horrors and difficulties, He has sent Jesus. This was love, infinite love. And Jesus, again in love, came and did everything that needed to be done to accomplish the Father's purpose. So much as in God lies, everything now is done.

The Epistle for today is a very beautiful section from the Sacred Scriptures, as you will have noticed when it was read; but were I not preaching Sunday for Sunday on the Epistles, I think I would have found it an even greater joy to preach on the Gospel for today. Since I am not preaching on it, I hope you will read it when you get home. It tells of a truly impressive instance in the ministry of Jesus. It is almost unbelievable what happened on that occasion. Jesus was very conscious that this was His final journey to Jerusalem. He knew it would be only a little while, and men would be cursing Him. He would be wrestling with the forces of hell in the Garden of Gethsemane. He would be dying on the accursed tree. All of this was vividly before His mind's eye. The curse and burden of humanity's whole guilt was weighing down on His soul. If ever any character in history had reason to think of himself and to forget everything and everybody else, it was Jesus at this particular time in His career. When He and His companions passed by the gates of Jericho, there was a poor blind beggar. The disciples passed him by, and others who were going up to Jerusalem for the festival occasion passed him by. When he heard the tramp, tramp, of feet, he asked, "What is this?" Somebody said, "Jesus of Nazareth is passing by." With a profound faith in his heart that Jesus, of whom he had heard, would not pass him by, but have some time and interest for him, this poor fellow cried out in his need. Human beings paid no attention. They said: "Be quiet. Jesus can't be bothered by a fellow like you now." Imagine what the disciples thought. Jesus had told them, "Now I am going up to suffer and die." They were overwhelmed with the idea. But Jesus, the One who was going to suffer and die, forgets about Himself. He thinks about this beggar. He stops the procession. He takes time out. He heals him and speaks to him a word of cheer and comfort. Such is the love of Jesus, the love which gave itself for you.

God wants you to have that love. He does not want you to go through life unhappy. Only last evening I was reading about a very successful and a very rich businessman. The article stated that no matter what he did, he never found satisfaction. No matter how successful he was, he never really could quiet down. And so it must be as long as sin is in your heart, and as long as you have not accepted God's solution for this problem. Well, God came in Christ to redeem you, and He succeeded in doing so.

The story of Lent is the story of Christ's redemptive work. If you have heard that story and if you believe it, cling to it. Come to the Lenten services. Read the Gospels so that your appreciation of God's love may grow and that you may learn how to apply that love to yourself more and more. If you never yet have learned this story, or if you have never yet accepted it, then do so now. You can be sure, outside God's love there can be no relief for your troubled heart. You will always remain an unhappy person, and nothing that can happen to you in this life can give you genuine joy and satisfaction.

Well, this story of God's love in Christ was the story about which Paul had written to the Christians at Corinth. In the first twelve chapters of that Letter he keeps them mindful of that wonderful truth. Now he speaks to them about the love wherewith they should respond to the love which God has shown to men. And so in the thirteenth chapter of his First Letter to the Corinthians he pens for us, by divine inspiration, this Psalm of Love.

THE GREATEST IS LOVE

He says: "Now there abide faith, hope, love, but the greatest of these is love." I wonder how many churchmen of how many denominations of our time would have dared to write that. I wonder! I think, if we had left it to men, to theologians, to write which was the greatest thing, theologians of one denominational group would have said: "Obedience, that is the greatest thing. The Church lays down the rules and regulations, and you obey." In another denomination they might have said: "Puritanical living. Avoid this; avoid that. Then you prove that you are a real Christian. That is the greatest thing." In another denomination they might have said: "Orthodoxy, that is the greatest thing." Others might have said: "Faith, heroic faith, that is the greatest thing." The Spirit of God didn't think so, for Paul wrote by divine inspiration. Paul said: "Now there abide faith, hope, and love, and the greatest of these is love."

He doesn't just make a bald statement, but He supports it. He says love is the greatest of all the Christian virtues. It is that because it is patterned after the behavior pattern of Jesus. When you read what Paul has to say, you cannot help thinking about Jesus. He is describing love. He says: "Love suffereth long and is kind; love envieth not; love vaunteth not itself, is not puffed up, doth not behave itself unseemly, seeketh not her own, is not easily provoked, thinketh no evil; rejoiceth not in iniquity, but rejoiceth in the truth; beareth all things, believeth all things, hopeth all things, endureth all things." Whom is he describing if not Jesus? Those are the qualities you find in the love, the character, and the ministry of Jesus.

Jesus was patient. If He hadn't been patient, He never could have stood it with those disciples of His. They must have annoyed Him tremendously. They were so slow in learning the Gospel. Even when Jesus was to be taken prisoner and nailed to the Cross, they still advised against it. After Jesus was in the grave, they still were not clear on just what had taken place. It was not until after Christ's resurrection and until He shed His Holy Spirit upon them in abundance on Pentecost that they finally saw the light and then courageously went forward to preach. Indeed, Jesus had infinite patience.

Jesus also was humble. He said: "The Son of Man came not to be ministered unto, but to minister." He did not hesitate to wash the disciples' feet or to stop for the healing of a blind beggar along the side of the dusty road leading from Jericho to Jerusalem.

Jesus trusted. Have you ever stopped to think how Jesus trusted when He entrusted to people like you and me the upbuilding of His kingdom? Think of it! He took twelve people, these disciples who were around Him, who failed Him on so many occasions, and to them He entrusted the task of building His Church here on earth. That is how He trusts you and me. Why? Well, because there is love in His heart. Love trusts. Love has patience. Love is humble. Perfect love made Jesus the model character of all time. He who knew no sin, who was spotless and as a Lamb without blemish, could be sacrificed for our sins. That is why you and I now should respond with love in our lives. Love is the greatest of Christian virtues because it is expressive of that which loomed largest in the heart of Jesus Himself.

LOVE IMPARTS MEANING TO OUR LIVES

Paul goes on to support this argument that love is the greatest of Christian virtues. He says it is love which invests everything else the Christian may think or do with meaning. He had previously spoken to the Corinthians about some of the fine gifts which God had bestowed upon the Church, the gift of speaking in tongues, the gift of prophecy, and others. Now Paul says they should remember that all of these gifts take their value and their meaning from love. If there is no love behind their use, then they are meaningless. He said: "Though I speak with the tongues of men and of angels and have not love, I am become as sounding brass or a tinkling cymbal. And though I have the gift of prophecy and understand all mysteries and all knowledge; and though I have all faith, so that I could remove mountains, and have not love, I am nothing. And though I bestow all my goods to feed the poor, and though I give my body to be burned, and have not love, it profiteth me nothing." You see, the most wonderful things people can do, do not mean a thing unless there is love behind them. The most eloquent preacher, the greatest theologian, the man with the strongest personality, could mount this pulpit Sunday after Sunday and address this audience, and it would not mean a thing to Almighty God unless that message came out of a heart that believed, out of a heart that had love, love for Him, love for those whom He redeemed. You can work yourself down to the bone in the women's society, on the Stewardship Committee, in the Sunday school, but unless you do what you do because you love your Savior and your church and your fellow men, don't do it! Because it doesn't mean a thing. You are being deceived. You are deceiving yourself. There is no real spiritual value in what you do. You may be the most generous giver to the church; when we come to the end of the year and make up our list, your name may stand at the head of the list; but if you give only for that reason, keep your money. It doesn't mean a thing to God. It is only when there is love motivating you in what you do that God has any pleasure in your deeds.

Apply that to your life. Look at the world of business. If you are the employer and I am the employee and grudgingly, after a long fight and a battle and all that sort of thing, finally you agree to give me better working conditions or a few cents more an hour, do you think that is going to inspire me? No, it is only going to do that when I think you love me as a fellow man and want to share honestly with me. A wife may busy herself in the home. She may spin the wool and weave the cloth for all of her children's clothes and her own, but if it is all just a stern duty and is not invested with love, it has no meaning. A husband can shower his wife with all sorts of gifts, but if it does not come out of a heart that is filled with love, it has no meaning. You see, it is love which

gives the deeds of life their true significance. That is why
love is the greatest virtue.

And finally, Paul says, love is the greatest because love
will endure. He says: "Love never faileth. But whether there
be prophecies, they shall fail; whether there be tongues, they
shall cease; whether there be knowledge, it shall vanish
away. For we know in part, and we prophesy in part. But
when that which is perfect is come, then that which is in part
shall be done away. . . . And now abideth faith, hope, love,
these three; but the greatest of these is love."

Today our knowledge is very piecemeal. We talk about
heaven as the Bible authorizes us to talk about heaven, but
all our talking about it is very inadequate, because it lies
beyond the scope of our experience. We cannot begin to
picture to ourselves the eternal majesty of God and the
infinite joys of heaven. It is not until we see Him face to
face that all of this will become real. Today we believe, but
tomorrow our faith will no longer be required because what
we believe and hope for will become a reality, and we shall
no longer know in part, but we shall know in entirety, in
fullness.

But love? Love goes on. It is love here, and it is love here-
after. It is always love. It does not change. That is the one
abiding quality in the Christian's heart and life. So the
greatest of these is love.

You realize that we find this to be true even in the life
and in the judgment of men. Who are the people whom the
world still honors, admires, looks to, with reverence and
grateful respect? Alexander the Great? No. We talk about
the man as being great because he had great armies and
developed a tremendous empire. We also know that he died

as a very young man because of his dissipations. He was cruel. He was immoral. Nobody loves him. Nobody respects him. But whom do we love? This week we observed the birthday of Abraham Lincoln. Abraham Lincoln—he was never rich. He never loved war. He hated it. He was not a highly educated individual. And yet the world around there are hearts that respond with sentiments of warmth when they hear the name of Abraham Lincoln. Why? Because he was a warmhearted man who had love within his soul. There was a spirit of love, of kindness, toward his fellow men. There have been great women who were renowned because of their physical attractions—Cleopatra and others. Does anybody love them? Does anybody admire them? No. All decent people think of them with aversion and disgust. But there was a Florence Nightingale. Just a simple soul, but one whose heart was filled with love, who went about doing good, who wanted to help people who were sick and in need. It is such as she who reap the harvest of universal respect and admiration.

And when you look at the galaxy of all the great names in history, there is still one name that is above every other name that can be named, the name of Jesus Christ. Why? Because He loved. He so loved that He gave Himself. This love, which should bring comfort to our hearts, which we should learn to apply with greater efficiency to all parts and needs of our lives, this love should be the pattern after which we seek to live our lives. This should be the power which enables us to express our love in relationship to God and in relationship to one another.

May God in His mercy be with us and help us so that each of us will understand—"The greatest of these is love."

Receive Not...in Vain

❖ ❖ ❖

We, then, as workers together with Him, beseech you also that ye receive not the grace of God in vain (for He saith: I have heard thee in a time accepted, and in the day of salvation have I succored thee. Behold, now is the accepted time; behold, now is the day of salvation!), giving no offense in anything, that the ministry be not blamed, but in all things approving ourselves as the ministers of God: in much patience, in afflictions, in necessities, in distresses, in stripes, in imprisonments, in tumults, in labors, in watchings, in fastings; by pureness, by knowledge, by long-suffering, by kindness, by the Holy Ghost, by love unfeigned, by the Word of Truth, by the power of God, by the armor of righteousness on the right hand and on the left, by honor and dishonor, by evil report and good report; as deceivers, and yet true; as unknown, and yet well known; as dying, and, behold, we live; as chastened, and not killed; as sorrowful, yet alway rejoicing; as poor, yet making many rich; as having nothing, and yet possessing all things.

II CORINTHIANS 6:1-10:

Today as God grants grace we want to consider the plea which Paul addressed to the Christians at Corinth and which we find recorded in the Epistle for this Sunday. Paul pleaded:

"We, then, as workers together with Him, beseech you also that ye receive not the grace of God in vain."

The Christians at Corinth had received the grace of God. They had heard the wonderful story of God's love. They knew what Jesus had done to save them from their sins. This grace which God had shown to the Christians at Corinth He has shown also to you and to me. He is showing it to us again today in this very service.

PAUL WORKED HARD TO BRING THE GOSPEL TO CORINTH

Paul wanted the Christians at Corinth to realize that this grace of God had been brought to them at great cost. He and His co-workers had spared no effort so that they might learn the story of God's mercy and fatherly kindness. He said that he had given offense in nothing, so "that the ministry be not blamed, but in all things approving ourselves as the ministers of God: in much patience, in afflictions, in necessities, in distresses, in stripes, in imprisonments, in tumults, in labors, in watchings, in fastings; by pureness, by knowledge, by long-suffering, by kindness, by the Holy Ghost, by love unfeigned, by the Word of Truth, by the power of God, by the armor of righteousness on the right hand and on the left, by honor and dishonor, by evil report and good report; as deceivers, and yet true; as unknown, and yet well known; as dying, and, behold, we live; as chastened, and not killed; as sorrowful, yet always rejoicing; as poor, yet making many rich; as having nothing, and yet possessing all things." Thus Paul described the heroic efforts of faith which had gone into the task of bringing God's grace to the people at Corinth. No labors had been spared. Everything had been suffered and endured, but the price was not too big to pay, because a big thing was to be achieved. These people living in what was then the most disreputable city in the world were to know that despite all their sins, God loved them, there was mercy in God's heart for each of them. They were to be the beneficiaries of God's grace in Christ.

Well, my friends, we cannot say that the ministry of this church has gone through all of the things Paul went through in order to bring you the grace of God in Christ. Perhaps you think not very much has gone into this. After all, the minister of today lives in a very comfortable home. He is provided with many of the comforts and conveniences of life. He is not thrown into jail. He is not exposed to all the things Paul was exposed to. Perhaps the grace of God came to you in an easier way than it came to Paul. Yet for us to say so would indicate a very superficial way of looking at it.

GREATER THAN THE WORK OF PAUL WAS THAT OF
JESUS AND THE HOLY SPIRIT

If you really want to know what it cost to bring the grace of God to you, then you must go way back to Calvary. That is where it started. You must see Jesus in Gethsemane and on Calvary enduring the infinite torments of hell, dying innocently as the atoning Sacrifice for your transgressions. That is where the Gospel foundations were laid. And from that day to this so much has been done to bring you the grace of God that many books could not begin to tell the story. When Jesus had completed His task; when His victory over all the enemies of your soul was a certainty, as manifested by His resurrection from the dead, then began the task of bringing to you the story of God's grace. Then the Spirit of God revealed this truth to individuals. These individuals committed it to writing. Even as in the days of the Old Covenant the messengers of the Most High who told of the Savior that was to come were inspired to transmit to all subsequent generations the record of that revelation, so now, when the Savior had come, the Spirit of God set Himself the task of providing the record of a completed redemption for you so that God's grace might reach your heart and soul.

When this record was completed by the inspired Evangelists and Apostles, from whose pen we have the Gospels and the Epistles of the New Testament, then the enemies tried to destroy that message. Many people gave their lives as martyrs for the protection, preservation, and transmission of this Gospel, that you might receive the grace of God. As the years passed by, devoted, God-fearing individuals hunched over these sacred writings and with minutest care copied them letter for letter, syllable for syllable, word for word, so that this message might be preserved for you. It mattered not how many individuals or how many organized groups of fanatical enemies or what mighty empires arose against this Word to destroy it and to keep from you the message of God's grace, God in His own wonderful way protected it. He saw to it that from generation to generation and from century to century it came down to our time.

EARNEST LABORS REQUIRED

It is altogether impossible for you or for me to have a completely adequate picture of all the work and the effort, the love, the devotion, the labor, that has gone into bringing God's grace to you so that today you can listen to the Word of God and to the saving Gospel of Jesus Christ. Many very eminent scholars have studied every letter in this Holy Book; some one part and some another part, some a book of the Old Testament, and some a book of the New Testament. They have dug up little pieces of broken pottery on which some poor person in the days of Jesus wrote one of Jesus' sayings, probably to send it on to bring comfort to the heart of a friend. They have studied papyrus writings just so that they might know what it is that God wants to say to us. They have taken scraps of the Holy Bible and larger portions as they have found them. They have taken the most ancient translations which have been made of this book. They have compared these texts and translations. Thousands and thousands of the most devoted and God-fearing scholars of the ages have given themselves to the study of this one book, of this one message, so that you might hear the story of God's grace. That is how God wanted it. Those were the efforts to which He has put Himself so that you might not fail to know how He feels in His heart toward you.

This work has gone on down to our own time. Only recently a new translation of the New Testament was published, and, by the way, a translation which has been very well received as a very acceptable piece of work. All of this forms the background, but it still is not the complete story. Then, after God by all of these labors had brought this message down to your day, He provided you with a God-fearing mother who had you stand at her knee while she told you this story and taught you to pray to this God of mercy and God of love. And then there was the Church, that group of organized Christians who established schools and seminaries so that men might be trained in these institutions and become prepared for the office of a Christian teacher or of the holy ministry so that they again in Sunday school, in school, in the confirmation class and from the pulpit could bring to you the story of God's grace in Christ. Think of it.

Paul wanted the Christians of Corinth to realize that it had cost some effort to bring them the Gospel. My friends, when the Lord addresses an appeal to you not to receive the grace of God in vain, then you ought to realize that behind that plea lies everything that happened in the redeeming work of Jesus, in His suffering and dying down through all the efforts made by the Spirit of God and the human agents whom He has employed so that you and yours can hear this message. If it were not for all that background, you would not know anything more about the Gospel of Jesus Christ than did Socrates or Plato. It would be a closed book for you.

WHILE GOD WOULD BRING, THE FORCES OF EVIL WOULD DENY, YOU GRACE

After Paul had made plain to the Christians at Corinth how desperately he and his co-workers had labored and how much they had suffered, he said, *"Don't receive this grace of God in vain."* Paul realized that there was such a possibility. These Christians at Corinth lived in a very wicked city. They themselves were sinners, and there was a possibility that all of love's labor and all of God's grace might be lost upon them.

False teachers followed wherever Paul went. When Paul told people: "You are saved by the blood of Jesus Christ," the false teachers came and said: "If you want to be saved, you must save yourselves. You must keep the Law of Moses. If you do not observe all the things Moses prescribed, you are not children of God, you are not going to get into heaven." So these people came and disturbed the converts whom Paul had won.

Then there was the world. It was a bad world. The lusts of the flesh were given free reign. Immorality was rampant in that city. "To Corinthianize" was an expression used throughout the Roman Empire to signify the worst and most abandoned kind of immorality. These Christians were living in such an environment. Naturally it appealed to their own flesh as it appealed to the flesh of the worldlings. They were prone to be easy in their moral standards. So Paul pleaded with them: "Don't let these false teachers, don't let this wicked world take you away from God. God has put forth such continuous efforts, and we tried so hard to bring you the Gospel and to give you a sample of Christian living in our own conduct and character. Now, don't throw it all away.— We beseech you that you receive not the grace of God in vain."

My friends, this is the plea which God would address to you this morning through me. "We beseech you also that ye receive not the grace of God in vain." So much has been done, as I tried very briefly and hurriedly to sketch for you, to bring you the message of God's grace. Don't receive it in vain. The possibilities are always present, first, because of your own heart. Some folks listen to the Gospel, but they do not want to have anything to do with it. They lock the door to their heart, and they throw the key away. They will not let the love of Christ get in because they do not want to have anything to do with the Savior. Either they are going to save themselves, or they do not want to be saved at all. To such you can preach the Gospel as long as you like, and they still will not receive it.

RECEIVE NOT IN VAIN

But there are those who do receive. They accept Jesus. They believe in Him. They try for a time to live like Christians, but then they give it up. It may be because they come under the influence of false philosophies. We have had some rather sad instances to record in that respect. We have had young people go out from our church to schools of higher learning who have there come under the influence of people who ridiculed religion, Christianity, with the result that young persons who went away from home as believing Christians came back as scoffing infidels. That is one way in which any of us can lose the grace of God. The world is continuously busy trying to impose its philosophy of unbelief and materialism upon us. You must not suppose for a single moment that you are altogether secure. So long as there is a breath of life in you, he who goeth about as a roaring lion seeking whom he may devour will try to put out the light of faith within your heart and plunge you once again into the darkness of sin and hopelessness. "We beseech you also that ye receive not the grace of God in vain."

Then, of course, there is the world with all of its lusts, its pride of life, and its sinful pleasures. There has never been a time in the whole history of the world when it has had more opportunities to deceive and mislead the children of God, who have received the grace and the mercy of God, than it possesses in our day. The world has so many avenues by which it can get at us now, through the printed page, through the movie, through the billboard, by very reason of the fact that with our automobiles and trains and airplanes we move about in a much larger circle than was true in foregone generations. Therefore the world has more opportunity to mislead us. There is danger in the present abundance of money. There is danger in the freely flowing floods of intoxicating liquors. There is danger in the loosening fiber of moral standards which prevail in a country such as ours. All of these things become a menace to our souls. That is why it is so important to have God address to us the appeal once addressed to the Christians at Corinth, "We beseech you also that ye receive not the grace of God in vain."

On top of this, we have all experienced the curse of one war and many of us the curse of two world wars. I am, frankly, gravely concerned, together with many of my fellow pastors in all Christian bodies, about the generation of today, which will be in control of life and affairs but a few years hence. The shock of the war has been tremendous. It has upset the lives of so many young people. It has cut right across the programs they had formed for their education, for their career in life, for marriage, and for the establishment of their homes. Shocks such as that often bring disastrous consequences. If it is true that people have lost their minds because they were so terribly shocked by immigrating from Europe to America and by the new circumstances of life which they found here, then imagine what the shock of war must have been to great numbers of young men and young women. Along with that shock has gone the fact that during wartime not only sweethearts, but also young husbands and wives were separated for long periods of time, with all the temptations attendant upon such separations. We have also suffered the spiritual losses occasioned by the cruelties of destroying peoples and countries by modern methods of warfare. And along with this has gone the assumed moratorium on morality which is universally accepted. It is not an accident if too many of the young men who were in the service are not taking up their place regularly in God's house on Sunday morning, if they are not taking hold of the work in the Kingdom of Jesus Christ, as we had so desperately hoped they would. These are all factors of life that must be reckoned with. And it is over against perils of this nature that we must understand the plea of God, when He talks to us and says, "I beseech you also that ye receive not the grace of God in vain."

PLEA APPLIES TO US

Let not one of us think that this plea applies to others, but not to us. No, if you have seen anything of life, then you know that he who thinks that he stands had better take heed lest he fall. There is nobody so good and nobody so secure that he can ever feel he needs no longer be on guard against the enemies of his soul. I have seen instances in which women who grew up from tiniest infancy in the most beautiful environment of a moral and spiritual nature but went the wrong way in the hour of temptation, to lose their faith and to abandon themselves to sin. You and I know of people who learned the story of God's grace in Christ from the earliest days in which they were able to understand the simplest words of human tongue. They were taught by God-fearing mothers how to utter reverently the name of Jesus Christ in simple prayers, and yet, despite all of the training, despite the spirit of godliness in their homes, despite the earnestness and consecration of Christian teachers and pastors, when they got out into the world, the fascination of money and the lure of fame and of power and the appeal to the lusts of their flesh as made by crude, gross sins of immorality became so powerful that some of the finest have gone the way of death. Ministers, men who were trained for the preaching of the Gospel of Jesus Christ, men whose job it was to deal with immortal souls in the name of the holy and merciful God, have in instances received the grace of God in vain. Their souls have been lost because they did not heed the plea of an understanding, anxious, merciful God.

And so I should like this morning to address to you Christians, living in a modern Corinth, surrounded with even greater dangers than were the Christians of Paul's day, this plea from the heavenly Father and from the Savior, who bled and died for you, "Receive not the grace of God in vain."

IMPORTANT TO POSSESS GRACE

This is important. It is important for you, for there is no other way of happiness in this world and no other way of salvation for the world which is to come. It is important not only for you, but for human society. The world is in a bad way, as you know. If there is to be light and hope for that world, it must come from the people who have stood at the foot of the Cross and who have looked into the loving countenance of the Christ on the accursed tree. Only as the light of love shines down from there into a world of hatred and greed and sin and brutality, can that darkness and ugliness be dissipated and the beauty of love and happiness take its place. So once again, "We beseech you also that ye receive not the grace of God in vain."

A Principle and Its Application

❖ ❖ ❖

Furthermore, then, we beseech you, brethren, and exhort you by the Lord Jesus, that as ye have received of us how ye ought to walk and to please God, so ye would abound more and more. For ye know what commandments we gave you by the Lord Jesus. For this is the will of God, even your sanctification, that ye should abstain from fornication; that every one of you should know how to possess his vessel in sanctification and honor, not in the lust of concupiscence, even as the Gentiles, which know not God; that no man go beyond and defraud his brother in any matter, because that the Lord is the Avenger of all such, as we also have fore-warned you and testified. For God hath not called us unto un-cleanness, but unto holiness.—I Thessalonians 4:1-7.

The Epistle for today presents for our consideration and study *a principle and a practical application of that principle to life.* The principle which God would urge upon us this morning by the words of our text is *the principle of spiritual growth.* You will all agree, I believe, it is important we should be reminded of this principle. Much of our spiritual life is lived with considerable complacency. We are all in-clined to think that we know almost everything that needs to be known about spiritual matters, that we have graduated as Christians. We do not remain constantly and consciously aware of the fact that growth, development, is a basic principle in the life of a Christian, as a matter of fact, a general principle of life.

GROWTH A PRINCIPLE OF LIFE

When a human being is born, he comes into this world as a tiny creature. God did not intend, however, that he should remain physically small. God has given to this newborn child the capacity of growth so that it can develop physically into the more mature stature of manhood or womanhood. This principle of growth applies also in the area of the intellectual. When a child is born, it has a mind. This mind, however, is still very undeveloped, but by gradual processes of experience and of instruction, that mind grows so that it becomes not only more fully informed, but also increasingly capable of sharp, clear, profound thinking. The more that mind is developed, the greater the capacity for thought. God has created the human so that he can grow.

THE PRINCIPLE OF SPIRITUAL GROWTH

What is true of man from the physical and intellectual point of view is equally true from the spiritual. It is this our Lord would impress upon us this morning. Paul wrote to the Christians at Thessalonica: "Furthermore, then, we beseech you, brethren, and exhort you by the Lord Jesus, that as ye have received of us how ye ought to walk and to please God, *so ye would abound more and more.*"

The Christians at Thessalonica were not to think of themselves as graduates, as completed Christians whose moral and spiritual life now was perfect and needed no further development. They were rather to think of themselves as individuals who were expected by God to grow in their spiritual and moral life. This principle of growth applies to every aspect of our spiritual life.

GROWTH IN CHRISTIAN KNOWLEDGE

You say: "Well, where should I grow? In what things should I develop?" There are many of them. God expects that *you and I should grow in our Christian knowledge*. Whenever you hear someone speak as though he knew all about Christianity and its teachings, you may well feel sorry for him. Anyone who is genuinely informed in matters of spiritual teaching, who has a fair store of Biblical knowledge, will never speak that way. The more informed the Christian is, the greater, the deeper, his spiritual understanding, the less inclined will he be to speak about it. He will know from the progress he has made how little he really does know. Whenever someone tells you that he is not interested in Christian doctrine and that he learned all that in school or Sunday school, you can be sure that you are dealing with a very superficial Christian. Only one who takes his religion in a very light and superficial way can have any such attitudes. Whenever you hear someone inquire rather naively, "Do you think it is important that we should be reading our Bibles all the time?" then you can know at once that you are dealing with an individual whose spiritual understanding is painfully limited. If his understanding were better, he would not speak in that way.

It is God's plan and purpose that we should grow, grow, first of all, in *our spiritual knowledge*. God has given us great truths, *the truth of sin*. Do you think you know the Bible doctrine about sin? Oh, no doubt you know there is such a doctrine, and no doubt you subscribe to it, but that doesn't mean that you have exhausted its meanng. If you study this doctrine as long as you live and just see how it operates in your own life and heart, how true it is of you, you will find your understanding growing. Your picture of sin and of your own spiritual need will become more and more clear with every passing day. You will get a fuller understanding so that as the days and the years pass by, you will come to stand more and more constantly and consciously and completely in the presence of your God with head hanging low. All pride, self-satisfaction, and spiritual conceit will be beaten out of you. You will not want to advance any arguments in your own behalf. You will be ready fully to join in the spirit of the one who said, "Just as I am, I come to Thee."

God tells us *about His love, about everything that Jesus has done for us.* If someone asked you if you knew about that, no doubt you would say, "Surely, I know all about that." Do you know all about that? Always feel sorry for the person who thinks he knows all about Jesus. There is so much beauty in the love of Jesus that you and I will never exhaust all its meaning. Every time you look at Christ, every time you take the Bible in hand and once again learn of God's mercy and love, some new facet of truth will be uncovered to you, and that gem will shine more brilliantly and sparkle with more fire than ever before.

What do you know about Holy Baptism? You were baptized. You are satisfied with the fact that you were baptized, but how much comfort does your Baptism bring you every day? How much of an inspiration is it to you? How often do you think about the fact that you were baptized? What practical significance does it actually have for you? You see, there is so much for you to learn about something that happened early in your life, something that you thought of as always taken care of. There is still so much to be learned if you are to get out of your Baptism what God intended for you to get.

What do you know about Holy Communion? Why, if we understood Holy Communion better, if we actually appreciated it as God wants us to appreciate it, do you think we would come to the Holy Supper only once or twice a year? We would with increasing frequency be eager and hungry guests at the Lord's altar. The reason why we can be so indifferent about so many of these things and treat our whole spiritual treasure store as though it were something very cheap and very common is that we know so little about it. Now, our Lord says: "Grow, abound more and more, let your understanding of spiritual truths increase."

GROWTH IN FAITH

This applies also to our faith. It is not only a matter of knowing, but it is also a matter of believing. *We should grow in our faith.* How much faith do you have? We speak our prayers, but only too often in a very superficial and mechanical way. Why? Why is it that we do not regard prayer as a wonderful privilege, as a marvelous experience each time we pray? Why is it so commonplace to us? Largely because we do not believe. We pray, but we really do not think anything is going to happen as a result of our prayers. Perhaps we are a bit fearful, a little bit too superstitious to just ignore and neglect prayer. We are afraid something might happen if we do not pray, but we really do not expect too much to happen if we do pray. And the reason why is that we do not believe. Our faith is so weak. We have so little confidence in God. We have quite a lot of confidence in ourselves, but so little confidence in God. This is so because we do not grow. We are satisfied. Whatever our faith is today, well, we hope it will be that tomorrow, a year from now, twenty years from now; just so long as we do not get worse, all is well.

If you would go through this community today, you would find a lot of people who are not going to be in God's house. They would assert that they believe, and yet they have had no living identification with the Church of God for years. They still deceive themselves into believing that all is well with their faith. Why?

If you and I would learn to commit ourselves into the keeping of God, if we would actually grow in this ability to lay everything into the lap of God and then by the grace of God to give ourselves to Him with whatever time, ability, and skill He has given us, oh, what a wonderful thing life would be! How much healthier we should be! If only we would believe! We wear our nervous systems out because we do not trust in God. We spend our nights sleeplessly because we do not trust God. We worry ourselves to death about our children, about our health, about our businesses, about a host of other things, because we do not trust God. We need to grow. We need to learn to trust God more and more.

FAITH AS MOTIVATING FORCE

Paul said to the Christians at Thessalonica, "Grow, abound more and more." They should learn how to use their faith and their knowledge. *It was to be the motivating power in their lives.* Why do you do the things you do? We come back to that question again and again. It is not hard to understand why the world does what it does. It wants profits. It wants power. It wants fame and glory and recognition. The motives of the world are clear as day. What are your motives? *You should learn to let the love of Jesus, the mercy of God, your faith, be the motive in your life.* You should be in business to express your love toward God. That is why you should take care of your household duties, your responsibilities as a mother. That is why you should apply yourself to your studies.

This is something we must learn. How many times in life do you say within yourself: "Now I am going to make this business deal, I am going to go to my job, or I will attend to this patient or this client, because Jesus loved me and here is my opportunity to express my gratitude in service to my fellow men"? How often do you figure in this way, and how often do you calculate: "Now, let me see; if I make this deal, my commission or my fee will be so much"? You see, we must grow. We are babes. Our Christianity is not the effective thing it ought be in our own lives or in the lives of other people because we do not grow. We stand still. We are not giving a very good demonstration of what Christianity should be. We are satisfied. The Lord says: "You have no right to be satisfied. There is a principle of growth that applies to your spiritual life. Now get busy, grow, abound more and more."

CHRISTIAN TRUTH AND LIFE

This applies also to *our use of Christian truth in application to our own everyday needs.* We are so inept when it comes to using our Christian faith for meeting the problems of everyday living. Here is a person who doesn't believe, and here is a person who does believe. Both of them must go to the hospital and have the same kind of operation. What difference is there between them? Sometimes no discernible difference at all, because the person who believes does not know what to do with his faith. He has never learned how to apply his faith to his life. He thinks his faith may have something vaguely to do with eternity and the hour of death. But he does not know how to use it in a practical way for life. This we are to learn.

We should grow also in the vigor and strength wherewith we win conquests over evil in our own lives. The life of the Christian is to be one of victory. It is always a life of struggle, but it should be a struggle in which the Christian comes out on top. We are to grow in our capacity to meet the enemy and to overcome him. Are you growing? Have you learned to cope with your temper, or do you still fly off with the same fury as you did a year ago, five years ago? How is it? Are you learning to control your tongue, or are you still the same spitfire you always were? Are you learning to say nice things instead of ugly things to your fellow men, or is it still giving you just as much pleasure as it did in the past to take them apart when you have an opportunity for doing so? Just how is it? It shouldn't be the same. You should be growing. Are you still that proud, self-satisfied, self-righteous, exceedingly sensitive person who, if touched and criticized just a little, is immediately hurt, mortally wounded? Or are you learning how to be kind and to see how many faults you have so that you will not be so hard on others? Are you growing, or are you standing still? The principle of God is clear: "Abound more and more." We should learn.

CHRISTIAN FAITH AND CHASTITY

Now, when Paul wrote *this great principle to the Christians at Thessalonica, he made one specific application of it.* Obviously this was an area of life in which the application needed particularly to be made in their case. The Christians at Thessalonica were living in a seaport. Thessalonica, like

Corinth, was one of the famous seaports. Well, like Corinth and other seaports, it had a great deal of shameful immorality and vice. The Christians at Thessalonica were exposed to these conditions of immorality. So when Paul lays down the principle that they were to grow, that they were to abound more and more, he finally comes to the point where he applies this to their own moral living. He tells them that they are to live as Christians, not as Gentiles, and therefore they are to practice chastity and not live in the immoralities which were common among the unbelieving.

If it was necessary to make this application of the principle that God's children should grow to the Christians in Thessalonica nineteen hundred years ago, I am sure you will agree that this is a day in which the same application needs to be made to our social conditions and to us as professing Christians. We are living in a world which, like Corinth and Thessalonica, has to a large degree abandoned all moral standards. The idea of chastity is absent from the hearts and minds of many of our contemporaries. Much of the literature which is produced in our country is deliberately designed to arouse lust and to inflame the hearts and minds of men with base passions. Many of the things that come out of Hollywood are deliberately intended to appeal to the baser side of human beings. So much of what passes for entertainment in the theater and in the night clubs is obscene— deliberately so. Recently a very well-known character in the American theater refused to accept the invitation to perform on a program in a night club in one of Chicago's best-known and largest hotels unless they would clean up their show. Think of it! Here was a night club in one of Chicago's very well-known and supposedly respectable hotels providing such unclean entertainment for its guests that a man whom they asked to come as an entertainer replied, "I will come, but not until you clean up your program."

BACKWASH OF WAR

The war has not helped us in this respect. The backwash of the war, of this war as of all past wars, has again been bad. Moral lines are always let down and loosened in time of war. People give themselves to immorality in the name of patriotism. Many young men and young women who felt that their day was passing by forgot about all social and moral restraints and lived as they pleased. Out of long separations have come many, many instances of infidelity. Thousands upon thousands of homes are being broken, and we, as the sons and daughters of God, live in that kind of atmosphere. It is now for us to grow. We are not to learn from the world how we should behave, but the world is to learn from us how it should behave. And God this morning would urge upon our hearts and our consciences the importance of living chaste, pure lives so that we respect the laws of conduct between the sexes as God Himself has given them to us.

This applies, first, to each of us individually. We all have evil hearts. It is as true of your heart as it is of mine that out of it come murder, adultery, fornication, as the Holy Scriptures say. We must conquer these hearts. We must never assume that we have learned, but each day we must learn yet better how to cope with that which is evil and how to encourage that which is good.

This applies to our home and family life. Inasmuch as we are the professed children of God, we should give first of all to our own sons and daughters a picture of a happy, beautiful family relationship. Then our neighbors should be able to see from us that there is something fine and clean and beautiful in our home and marriage. We must not assume that we have learned everything. No. We must grow. We must learn better day by day how to do this so that God may be glorified, so that our own lives may be enriched, and so that human society may be benefited by us as members of it.

CHRISTIAN INFLUENCE

Yes, we must make our influence felt in society at large. Perhaps you saw the newspaper account which told that a Catholic priest took his young people out of a certain organization identified with a well-known baseball club because a very important member of that club made himself guilty of conduct unbecoming a decent man or woman. We must give that priest credit for what he did. Think what would happen if all the Christian men and women in this country were to say: "I will not buy a book which was written for the purpose of disseminating smut." It would not take very long before we professing Christians would bring every book publisher to his knees. He would not dare to publish smut. If sixty million professing Christians in the United States of America would say: "We are not going to buy smutty and obscene literature," the people who write that kind of stuff would starve, and the people who print it would go out of business. Just think what would happen if we would say: "We are not going to keep adulterers in beautiful castles and on expensive yachts, and we are not going to put costly furs and beautiful diamonds on adulteresses in Hollywood who bring out the smut that is intended to tear down the moral standards of decency which we are trying to teach to our children." How long do you think those people could go on if sixty or sixty-five million people in this country would not patronize the movies which showed immoral pictures?

You see, we do not even establish a level. The world can give us whatever it wants, and we pay for it. Some of you folks are ready to go out and spend more to have somebody provide you with two and a half hours of immoral entertainment than you are ready to give to God's house for the privilege of listening to the Word of eternal truth. Think of it! That is how weak we are. That is how low our moral standards are. So it is with reference to this particular thing that God now would have us make application also of the principle "Grow, abound more and more."

Think it over. Talk it over in the circle of your own family. See what by prayer and earnest thought you can do with this great principle in your own life.

Children of Light

❖   ❖   ❖

Be ye, therefore, followers of God, as dear children; and walk in love, as Christ also hath loved us, and hath given Himself for us an offering and a sacrifice to God for a sweet-smelling savor. But fornication and all uncleanness or covetousness, let it not be once named among you, as becometh saints; neither filthiness, nor foolish talking, nor jesting, which are not convenient, but rather giving of thanks. For this ye know, that no whoremonger, nor unclean person, nor covetous man, who is an idolater, hath any inheritance in the Kingdom of Christ and of God. Let no man deceive you with vain words, for because of these things cometh the wrath of God upon the children of disobedience. Be not ye, therefore, partakers with them. For ye were sometimes darkness, but now are ye light in the Lord; walk as children of light (for the fruit of the Spirit is in all goodness and righteousness and truth).
EPHESIANS 5:1-9.

The words of the Epistle for today were originally addressed to the Christians who lived in the city of Ephesus. Paul called these Christians *"children of light."* He reminded them, however, that there had been a time when they had

not been children of light. When Paul first met them, they
were in the dark. They had some natural knowledge of God
and some natural understandng of right and wrong, but they
did not know who the true God was. They did not know
how to cope with the problem of sin. The answer to these
questions had never been brought to them; so they were in
the dark.

THE COMING OF LIGHT

Then came Paul, the ambassador of God and of Jesus
Christ. He brought them light. He told them not only about
sin so that they could recognize more clearly the greatness
of their spiritual need, but he told them most particularly
about Jesus and all that He had done for them to work out
the salvation of their souls. He told them how the mercy of
God in Christ had paid for all of their transgressions. The Spirit
of God used the message which Paul brought to them,
opened their eyes, and gave them light. As the light was
given to them and they with their hearts began to trust in
this Jesus as their Savior from sin, they became the children
of light. Thus, when Paul wrote his Letter to the Ephesians,
he could call these people, who once had been in darkness,
children of light, who now knew the true God and believed
in Christ, whom He had sent.

Your story and my story is like that of the Ephesians.
When you and I were born into this world, we came as
people who were in the dark. We had a natural knowledge
of God. We had some understanding of what was right and
what was wrong, but it was not until God came to us with
His special revelation as contained in His holy Word and as
expressed in the divine Sacraments, it was not until the
Spirit of God began to work in our hearts that we became
children of light. As God told you the story of Himself and

His love for you and of all that Jesus has done for you, He dissipated the clouds of darkness and allowed the light of divine truth to shine in. When you accepted Jesus and said, "This is my Lord, who has redeemed me," then you became a child of light. God took you out of darkness and brought you out here "in the know," as it were, in the light, where you knew your Savior and Redeemer.

LIGHT DIVINE

If you are still in the dark, if you have never yet seen this light, or accepted Jesus as your Savior, then, as an ambassador of Christ, I would like to invite you now to do so. There is no reason why you should be in the dark, why you should wonder as to the future, why you should be in ignorance about God or about God's attitude toward you, or about the manner in which you can be freed from sin and enter into communion with God. Jesus has done everything that needed to be done also for you. Only believe this. Build your hope on what He has done, and then you need not be worried about your sins any more. Then you, too, will see the light of divine love shine, and you will know that there is a promise waiting which goes beyond this day and this world.

CHILDREN OF LIGHT SHOULD LIVE AS SUCH

Now, addressing these children of light, Paul had a special message for them. Because they were children of light, it was expected of them by God that *they should walk as children of light*. Just what that meant Paul presented to them under two aspects. On the one hand, he told them *what they should not do*, inasmuch as they were the children of light, and then he told them *what they should do as children of light*. He said: "But fornication and all uncleanness or covetousness, let it not be once named among you, as becometh saints; neither filthiness, nor foolish talking, nor jesting, which are not convenient."

WHAT CHILDREN OF LIGHT SHOULD NOT DO

These people were living in Ephesus. That was the biggest city to which Paul had come up to that time. Ephesus was the center of the cult of Diana. Diana was the goddess of fertility. The very exercises of worship associated with the cult of Diana invited people to live in the vilest kinds of immorality and sins of uncleanness of every description. So vice and sin, lust and shame, were rampant in Ephesus. These Christians lived in Ephesus. They breathed the very atmosphere of this city. They were human beings. Their hearts, too, were prolific producers of evil thoughts. The temptation to do as the worldlings did in the city of Ephesus was always present with them. So Paul pleaded with them to fight these obscenities, not to do as the children of the world were doing. They were the children of light.

Then he reminded them that there was a special reason why they should avoid these things. He said: "For this ye know, that no whoremonger, nor unclean person, nor covetous man, who is an idolater, hath any inheritance in the Kingdom of Christ and of God. Let no man deceive you with vain words, for because of these things cometh the wrath of God upon the children of disobedience." He reminded them that these particular sins, which were so prevalent in the city of Ephesus, carried their own retribution along with them. No individual and no people could live a life of moral abandonment without bringing upon themselves the wrath of God.

This is something very important for us. We are perpetually living amidst the spirit of Corinth and of Ephesus. These lustful sins of the flesh have lost none of their popularity, although nineteen hundred years have intervened from Paul's day until this. They have at all times and in all lands been the most popular and the most powerful and the most destructive of all sins. When you read the history of ancient peoples, you do not have to pursue your studies very far before you discover that one people after another was buried in the grave of lustfulness. People could withstand enemies, they could withstand famine, storms, epidemics of one kind or another, which in the days of the past would level whole countrysides. One nation after another could withstand experience of that kind, but there is one thing no nation has ever been able to withstand, and that is the ultimate decline of their morals. When chastity went out and unchastity came in, that nation was doomed. No words could begin to describe the heartache, the immorality, the physical, mental, and spiritual suffering which is in the United States of America as of this morning because of the sins of uncleanness. You could go from one hospital to another, from one institution to another, and you could go into many haunts and many homes, and you could find over and over again the terrific price men pay because of the sins of uncleanness.

PREVALENCE OF SMUT

How prevalent uncleanness is you can see from the type of humor which is purveyed in our day. People on the stage often vie with one another in the effort to become ever more and more smutty in the kind of jokes which they tell. Apparently something like that was happening in Ephesus, too, because Paul said, "Neither filthiness, nor foolish talking, nor jesting, which are not convenient." If there had been no occasion for so writing, he would not have done so. Paul did not tell them never to laugh. No, he was only warning against a certain kind of joke, the kind of jokes which even the radio entertainers are trying to bring on the air in ever bolder measure, the kind of thing that cartoonists even try to introduce into the so-called comics drawn for the consumption of the American youth. Unblushingly they try to make a lustful appeal. You and I are living in this world. This is the atmosphere we breathe. Now, God would say to us this morning: "While you live in that kind of an environment, you are not to be a part of it, because you are the children of light. Walk in the light. Don't go over there, into the areas of darkness where sin and the forces of evil carry on their nefarious and soul-destroying work; but you stay over here, in the area of light. And don't let anybody deceive you with vain words."

It has become so common in our day to teach people that they should not in any way repress, or inhibit, their desires, for this would be hurtful to their personalities. It has become almost a matter of religious faith with many people that the only way they can be happy is to give free rein to whatever the desires of their heart may be. If it is the desire of their heart, it is their perfect privilege to gratify it. Those are vain and deceptive words. They are a damnable lie, of which God does not approve. And anyone who makes such sentiments the guide of his life is bound someday to discover that he has been lied to. Only heartache and suffering can result from a violation of God's will in the matter of chastity.

COVETOUSNESS

But there is another matter which was also a grave danger to these children of light who then lived in the great city of Ephesus, and that was the sin of covetousness. Paul said: "But fornication and all uncleanness *or covetousness*, let it not be once named among you." He said: "For this ye know, that no whoremonger, nor unclean person, *nor covetous man, who is an idolater, hath any inheritance in the Kingdom of Christ and of God."*

We get a little insight into the covetousness of the Ephesians from the Book of Acts. It was at Ephesus where Paul experienced one of the most violent riots that was ever called against him. Paul was a very successful mission worker in this great city. Since it was the center of the cult of Diana, there were many craftsmen who worked in silver and gold and who made and sold images of their favorite goddess. When people became Christians, they no longer bought these statues. So these gold and silversmiths were no longer doing a good business. Hence they wanted to get rid of Paul. They would rather fill their pockets with money than receive the truths of God. They would rather keep other people in the degrading belief in the goddess of fertility than lose their business and have them worship at the foot of the Cross in the presence of the Christ. So you see, covetousness, to make more and more money, was the spirit of the Ephesian people. The Christians lived in that atmosphere. What they saw the children of the world do, they, too, were tempted to do. They wanted to do what the others did. Paul said: "These people are not children of light, they are idolaters. Money is their god. Now, that is not what you want. You are children of light. Walk in the light. Don't walk in darkness. Don't worship mammon, one of the world's most popular idols."

GREED

If it was important for Paul to say this nineteen centuries ago to children of light who lived in Ephesus, imagine how important it is that it should be said to children of light who live in one of the most bustling cities of the world, who live in the very heart of a great nation upon which God has poured out material wealth in endless abundance. Here we are living in the city of Chicago, the city of "go," where people chase the almighty dollar with a vim and vigor that fairly astounds people in other parts of the earth. This is where we live. Don't think for one moment that the spirit of the world does not affect you. No, when you see how the world greedily goes after the things of this life and of this world, you are invited and impelled and urged by their example and by the desire of your own heart to do as they do.

Out of this come many of our problems of today. We wouldn't have all of this fighting between capital and labor if there were not so much greed in industry. One day it is the man who hires people who is not satisfied with what he gets. Then there comes another day, and then the man who is hired sits at the top of the heap, and he wants to go on and get more and more. No matter what he gets, he still is not satisfied. And so, then, out of this greed and out of the desire of one to take from the other, so that he may get what he can, comes strife. Out of this comes one of our problems. Since it is a world in which mammon is so popular, where so many altars are erected to the worship of material things, you and I, as the children of light, need to be warned, lest we, too, bend our knees at these altars, turn away from the altar of the true God to the altars of false gods, and give our hearts to that which never can make us happy or bring us peace. "This ye know, that no . . . idolater hath any inheritance in the Kingdom of Christ and of God. Let no man deceive you with vain words."

This whole philosophy of our day, that human problems are mostly economic problems and that all our difficulties would be taken care of if only we could give people enough of this world's goods, is all a lie. Yes, it is true, we should share, and it is imperative that those who are hungry be fed, that those who are naked be clothed, and that those who are without shelter be housed. That is God's plan and purpose, but it is not true that any human anywhere in this world ever has gotten satisfaction and true happiness out of material things. He who worships mammon loses the peace of God and his place in the Kingdom of God.

WHAT CHILDREN OF LIGHT SHOULD DO

So Paul, writing to the Christians at Ephesus, said: "Now, remember, once you were in darkness. You did not know what the truth was, but now you are children of light; so avoid these things and, instead, do this: As the children of light, walk in the light." "Now are ye light in the Lord; walk as children of light (for the fruit of the Spirit is in all goodness and righteousness and truth)." "Be ye, therefore, followers of God." Really what it says is: "Be ye, therefore, *imitators* of God." That is the way the new translation has it. "Be ye, therefore, imitators of God, as dear children; and walk in love as Christ also hath loved us." These people at Ephesus were no longer to be a part and parcel of the world. Their life was now to be lived in service to God. Christ had loved them. They were now to hate the things from which He had bought them free and devote themselves to those things for which He had purchased them: love and truth, goodness and righteousness.

This is our call. You as a child of light are asked by God to be an imitator of Him. As He has shown love to you, so should you show love to God by showing love to your fellow men. There is no escape from this matter of love in the life of the Christian; and if he is to live a life of love and imitate God, then his must be a life of goodness and righteousness and of truth. Everything that is false must be hated. Everything that is wrong, that is unjust, that is in rebellion against God, that is destructive of human happiness, of human right, and of human majesty, should be put aside, and love should find its expression.

Each of us has a circle in this world within which we live out our lives. You have your own particular sphere in which you live and operate from day to day, from week to week, as you continue your journey through life. Wherever you are, you are to be a child of light. You are never in the dark. You know that God loves you, you know that Jesus redeemed you, and you know what He would have you do to show your gratitude and your appreciation. Now it is for you as a child of light to represent in this world that which is righteous, that which is true. As a child of light, you cannot escape that social responsibility. When you profess to be a child of light, but then live as one who is in darkness still, you deny your position, and you forsake your Lord. But when you live as a child of light, then you are a torchbearer. Then you can be distinguished from those who are in darkness. People can tell from the very way in which you talk and act that you are a follower of Jesus, that you have certain standards of conduct which the children of this world do not have. They do some things you will not do. They support some things which you must oppose and condemn.

Here we are in the season of Lent, the third Sunday in this holy season, and this is the earnest exhortation which God addresses to each of our souls: "Be ye, therefore, followers of God, as dear children. Now are ye light in the Lord. Walk as children of light."

Two Kinds of Religion

❖ ❖ ❖

Tell me, ye that desire to be under the Law, do ye not hear the Law? For it is written that Abraham had two sons, the one by a bondmaid, the other by a freewoman. But he who was of the bondwoman was born after the flesh; but he of the freewoman was by promise. Which things are an allegory; for these are the two covenants: the one from the Mount Sinai, which gendereth to bondage, which is Agar. For this Agar is Mount Sinai in Arabia and answereth to Jerusalem which now is and is in bondage with her children. But Jerusalem which is above is free, which is the mother of us all. For it is written: Rejoice, thou barren that bearest not; break forth and cry, thou that travailest not; for the desolate hath many more children than she which hath an husband. Now, we, brethren, as Isaac was, are the children of promise. But as then he that was born after the flesh persecuted him that was born after the Spirit, even so it is now. Nevertheless, what saith the Scripture? Cast out the bondwoman and her son, for the son of the bondwoman shall not be heir with the son of the free-woman. So, then, brethren, we are not children of the bond-woman, but of the free.—GALATIANS 4:21-31.

Our text is not easy to understand. May the Holy Spirit use our meditation to make clear its meaning to all present, for Jesus' sake. Amen.

We are all aware that there are many religions in this world. You may not be so aware that all of these religions fall into two classes—two and two only—no more, no less. The one is the Christian religion, and the other takes in all of the non-Christian religions.

PAUL—PROPONENT OF CHRISTIANITY

Paul, the author of our text, had been in the Roman province of Galatia, preaching Christianity. He had brought his message to Jewish-Gentile audiences in some of the more populous Galatian communities. He had told his audiences about the redeeming love of God. He had met the realities of life head on. He helped them realize that they were sinners who needed help. Then he told them about the infinite love of God in Christ, who had come into this world as a Child, grown to manhood, who had assumed all of their sins and burdens, and then given His own life as an atoning sacrifice to wipe out all of their guilt and shame. Many of these people believed the message of Paul. They accepted the Gospel of Christ. They were happy in this new-found faith, in this assurance of divine love and heavenly mercy. But Paul wasn't the only one in this world who preached. He preached Christianity, but there were others who preached the other kind of religion.

ENEMIES OF CHRISTIANITY

When Paul left a community, these enemies of Christianity followed. It was much like a political campaign in which two candidates schedule their speeches in the same general communities, and the one tries to follow and undo whatever the other may have done before him. So these people followed Paul into all of the communities into which he had gone. And they spoke something like this to the converts of

Paul: "Don't you believe that man. What he tells you simply isn't true. You can't be a child of God merely by believing in Jesus. Paul is trying to give you an easy way to heaven. He's deceiving you. If you really want to be saved, there's only one way in which it can be done, and that is by working out your own salvation."

When the converts of Paul heard this message, they became confused. The poor people didn't know any more what they should believe. Should they rely upon Jesus for the salvation of their souls, or should they rely upon the things which they were doing themselves or were able to do themselves for their own redemption and salvation?

Paul learned of their difficulty. He also knew, of course, how tremendous would be the pull in the direction of this non-Christian religion. Paul had had that kind of religion himself in the earlier years of his life. He knew that was the religion of every man as he is born into this world. So he wrote them the Letter from which our text is taken, the Letter to the Galatians. And he tried to explain it to them. The method which he used is not one which is familiar to us in modern times. He harked back to a Bible story which had happened about 2,000 years before Jesus was born. He employed the method of allegory. Allegory is a form of speech in which you say one thing but illustrate another. Paul used the story of Abraham and his family life as an allegory.

AN ALLEGORY

Abraham was the father of all believers. Abraham was married to a beautiful woman whose name was Sarah. God had promised Abraham that out of his loins should come the Messiah. Years passed, and Sarah remained barren and childless. Both Abraham and Sarah began to worry whether God's promise was going to be fulfilled. When Sarah had lost all hope of motherhood, she finally gave her slave, Hagar, to Abraham so that he might have a child with her. Hagar conceived and brought forth a son, whose name was called Ishmael. Hagar was a slave, and her son was not the legitimate heir of his father. Late in life, according to the promise of God, Sarah conceived and brought forth Isaac. "Now," said Paul to his readers of that day, "this is an allegory. Hagar represents the non-Christian religions."

At first it certainly had every appearance as though Hagar's position were a very enviable one. After all, she had a child, Sarah did not—which in those days was thought of a great deal more seriously by women than is true today. It seemed as though all the benefits were coming Hagar's way and as though Sarah were going to be the poor, lonely, unloved, and heartbroken individual for whom God was not going to fulfill the beautiful promise which He had made. As was true of Hagar, so Paul wanted these people in Galatia to realize it was also true of the kind of religion his opponents were preaching.

A POPULAR BUT UNSATISFACTORY RELIGION

When you go to a man and give him a long list of rules and you say to that man: "If you will observe all of these rules, then you will be a child of God, then you will earn heaven for yourself, then all will be well with your soul"—I say, when you go to a man and you give him such a religion, that all sounds very impressive. It sounds as though you really were a holy person; as though you really meant business about this matter of religion; as though you were not going to make religion easy for anybody—and if he wants to have religion, he had better go to work.

People who preach that kind of religion always make a tremendous impression. They sound so holy, and they seem so good. You see that was Christ's trouble in His day. He didn't preach that kind of religion, but the Scribes did. And so when people began to compare the Scribes, with all their many rules and regulations, with the kind of religion Jesus was preaching, the Scribes seemed a whole lot holier than Jesus ever had. "Why," they said, "that man companies with harlots and publicans. He eats and drinks with sinners." They couldn't understand that kind of religion. Just so these people who had come to the Galatians had made a great impression on them, and by way of comparison Paul didn't seem to be nearly so serious-minded about religion. He hadn't given these people a long list of rules and then said: "Now, do this, and then everything will be all right."

Paul reminded them that if it seemed at first as though Hagar had by far the better of the deal, there came a day when Hagar discovered that her son Ishmael was not the heir of Abraham and that she was not the wife of Abraham and that they were dismissed from the house when she became arrogant in her attitude over against Sarah, the true wife, and over against her son Isaac. And so Hagar and Ishmael fell short of achieving their purpose. The inheritance did not come to them. They were driven out.

That is the dastardly thing about all non-Christian religions. It doesn't make one little bit of difference how much they may impress people and how holy they seem to be and how serious. In the final analysis they don't give the human heart what it needs. You see, if you were given the Ten Commandments, the Sermon on the Mount, and a host of other rules and regulations and then told: "Now, do this, and then all will be well with your soul," you might try. Paul had tried it. He had failed. He had discovered it couldn't be done. No matter how you tried, you would never succeed in doing the thing perfectly. You would always fall short, and it would be that element of deficiency which would leave a doubt in your heart. You could never come altogether to the goal. No matter how close you came, you would never reach it. That is the damnable and the deceptive part of all such religions. They leave men out there in an area of uncertainty. They can never provide real peace for the human heart.

And it was this truth which Paul wanted to get over to the readers of his Letter in the Christian congregations of Galatia. Now, my friends, this is something you and I must understand. Until you understand that, your spiritual life is always going to be in a state of confusion. So long as you still think you are going to work it out, you are always going to fall short.

TWO KINDS OF IDEAS

This has significance not only for your personal spiritual life, this is a truth of tremendous significance for all of human society. Today we have two kinds of ideas, political, economic ideas, diametrically opposed to each other. The one is the idea of Karl Marx, the father of Communism. Karl Marx said in effect: "All human ills arise out of the economic system which prevails throughout the world. If we can succeed in overthrowing this economic system and giving to all men an equal share in this world's goods, then we shall not even require a government. In between the time of the overthrow and the actual achievement of this universal communistic system we may need a dictatorship, but eventually the dictatorship will wilt and die—it will just dry up by itself, because it will no longer be necessary." He assumed that the human heart was capable of doing something perfectly good. He thought all the ills came out of a system and didn't understand that they came out of the human heart.

So he thought the only thing you had to do was to change the system, and then all of life would be sweet, serene, and beautiful. You and I know that isn't true, and the reason why it isn't true is that the ills of men, even the evil systems which may exist in one or another area of life, finally have been devised by the human heart. So the problem of man lies not in a social situation, but in the evil which is in the heart of man himself. That is why this kind of religion will not satisfy, and that is why any system of economics or government based on such a theory never can succeed.

Well, the great idea which is standing in diametrical opposition to Communism is capitalism. We have a host of people in our country and perhaps in other countries, too, who are of the opinion that you need only give the human being free reign. If you will let all the people of America carry on in their respective businesses as they want, everything will work itself out, because there are within society the necessary checks and balances to make it all function. Now, of course, that isn't true. The truth is that if you will allow people to proceed as they like, the evil in the human heart is going to express itself, and the people who are strong and mighty are going to take advantage of the people who are not so strong and mighty. And anyone who talks about that way of looking at life as a solution for human ills is forgetting that the evil does not lie in a system, but in the hearts of men who are trying to make a system operate.

THE CHRISTIAN RELIGION

Paul made plain to the Galatians that they could never be free people, they could never find real peace for their hearts and freedom from their fears so long as they would allow themselves to be enslaved under a religion of rules and laws which would say to them: "This is what you must do; and if you do it, all will be well; and if you don't do it, it's too bad for you." "Now," he said, "if Hagar represents that kind of religion, Sarah represents, or symbolizes, the Christian religion." She was the legitimate wife of Abraham. She gave birth to Isaac, the child of promise, and here you have love and loveliness expressing itself as you have it in the Gospel of Christ. According to God's promise, Jesus came. In His infinite love He had compassion on all men. He atoned for the sins of every sinner and now offers grace as a free gift of divine love to everyone who will accept it. Man is saved not by the deeds of the Law, but by grace, through faith in Jesus Christ. This is the *only* answer which takes *complete* care of human hearts. Here there are no deficiencies. There are no unattended areas of spiritual need. The gift of God is a free gift. It is available to all, and it covers the whole problem of spiritual need. So Paul warned them: "Don't you let anybody take this religion from you."

You can see how easy it is to attack Christianity. It's a free gift of love. People have said, in the first place, that does not do justice to man, and, most of all, they have been worried that it makes religion much too easy for human beings. They have said: "Any such offer of forgiveness and grace is a wide-open invitation to a life of moral indifference and carelessness. Why should anybody worry how he lives if after all he doesn't work out his own salvation, but gets it as a free and gracious gift from God?"

Paul reminded his readers: "Don't you let momentary appearances deceive you. It looked for a time as though Hagar were going to be the winner, but she wasn't. She lost with her son Ishmael. But Sarah received the promise, and Isaac was the heir of his father, Abraham, and it was through that line and strain the Messiah finally came and God's people were multiplied and became the bearers of Messianic assur-

ances. So it is with the Christian who clings to Christ as his
Redeemer. There he has not only a partial answer to his
needs, but a complete answer."

PERFECT PEACE

When you accept Jesus, then there are no dark corners in
your heart. The whole heart becomes illuminated with divine
love. Then you have full peace, the kind of peace the world
cannot give. Just how inexpressibly significant this is for
human beings I would imagine the psychiatrists of today
could tell us perhaps better than anybody else. They are
learning from their daily experiences with men that human
beings are in no greater need than that of inner peace, a
quiet conscience, freedom from fear. Because people are
being driven by their fears, by their sense of guilt, they are
so indescribably miserable and unhappy. They can't settle
down to be quiet, to enjoy the fine things that God has given
them in this life, and, on the other hand, to share with others
graciously and generously in those fine things. But when the
peace of God comes into the heart, then, first of all, you have
that perfect answer to the needs of your soul, and with that
answer there begins to develop within your heart a desire to
say "Thank you." The more you come to realize and appreciate what God has given you in Christ, the more determined
you will be to show in your everyday life that you are grateful for this wonderful and unmerited gift of heavenly love.

Here is something that lifts life above the level of sordid
greed and selfishness. So long as I live under a religion of
rules, I do good only because I am trying to earn something
for myself. The minute I live under the religion of Jesus
Christ, I do good because I love Christ. I don't have to earn
anything for myself. My Lord has earned it for me. And so

life is being lived on a higher level, the universally recognized higher level of love, unselfishness.

So you see, in the religion of Jesus you not only have an answer which is complete and which takes care of all questions and doubts for life and for death, for time and for eternity, but you also have an approach to the great social issues of our day. Communism is not going to answer humanity's problems. If you had a human family to deal with in which all hearts are perfect, we could probably make such a system work; but to assume that it is going to work merely by overthrowing an existing order is worse than silly, because it fails to recognize the evil that is in the human heart.

No, if human society is to be improved and the relationships among men are to be made friendlier and mutually more helpful and beneficial, then, first of all, we must get the message of Christ into human hearts so that there will be an ever-growing number of people who will try, as the Spirit of God gives them the ability, day by day to express love in their relationship to their fellow men. The meanwhile, however, we will always realize that this thing cannot and will not be achieved perfectly, because they who are Christians will not be perfect, and there will always be need for a controlling power, for which God in His infinite wisdom made provision when He instituted government. The greater the degree of love in human hearts, the less the need for government. The greater the degree of selfishness in human hearts, the greater the need for government.

So you see, we really are face to face with the problem, do we want to work for a world in which an autocratic, all-governing all-controlling State is going to write the detailed rules and regulations for our lives, or are we going to live for a world of freedom in which there will be a minimum of government with a maximum of love in the human heart? It is all going to be determined, in the final analysis, by the successes or failures, the victories or defeats, of the cause of Jesus Christ. Paul put it to his people in the form of an allegory. I hope I am succeeding somewhat in putting it to you in language of today so that you can see it for your own hearts, to have personal peace and a driving, throbbing, motivating force of love within your souls for the living of a beautiful personal life and for an understanding of what the world at large needs so that you can recognize the significance of Christianity for human society as such, not only for eternity, but for the life and the world that now is.

May God to that end be with us and help us, give us light and understanding, for Jesus' sake. Amen.

For Life and for Death

❖   ❖   ❖

But Christ being come an High Priest of good things to come, by a greater and more perfect tabernacle, not made with hands, that is to say, not of this building; neither by the blood of goats and calves, but by His own blood He entered in once into the Holy Place, having obtained eternal redemption for us. For if the blood of bulls and of goats, and the ashes of an heifer sprinkling the unclean, sanctifieth to the purifying of the flesh, how much more shall the blood of Christ, who through the eternal Spirit offered Himself without spot to God, purge your conscience from dead works to serve the living God? And for this cause He is the Mediator of the new testament, that by means of death, for the redemption of the transgressions that were under the first testament, they which are called might receive the promise of eternal inheritance.—HEBREWS 9:11-15.

CHRISTIANITY RELEVANT

A man with whom I was corresponding wrote me one day, "Yours is a religion for death." He wanted to say that your religion and my religion was good to have when it was time to die, but that it had no particular relevance to our everyday lives. We must admit, I believe, that a great many professed Christians would give almost anyone the idea that this is true. So often even we who profess to be followers of Jesus think of our religion as something that will stand us in good stead when we are called out of this world, but beyond that we are frequently tempted to think of it as a hindrance rather than a blessing. I find boys and girls in the confirmation class sometimes expressing themselves to the effect that one really would be better off for this world if he were not a Christian. They get an idea that Christianity places all sorts of inhibitions upon a person. A person who is not a Christian can live out his life and do virtually what he pleases to do, whereas the Christian finds all kinds of hindrances in the way which hamper and restrain him. So if a man standing on the outside, looking in, gets an idea that Christianity is a religion for death and not for life, we cannot really blame him too much, but certainly we cannot agree that such a view of Christianity is correct. The truth is that all those who think of Christianity as a religion for death have only a very fractional understanding of Christianity, if they have any understanding at all.

If you and I look at the words of the Epistle for today, then we understand that Christianity is both for life and for death. This text is taken from a Letter that was written to the Hebrews. We cannot be sure who the author of this Letter was. Many have ascribed it to the Apostle Paul, and others have said: "No, it was not written by Paul." But that is not so important as it is to know that it is a revelation of God. This revelation was given for the express purpose of convincing the Hebrew people that Jesus was the Messiah who was promised to them. That explains the Old Testament references which you find in this particular text.

RELIEF FOR OUR CONSCIENCE

When we look at this text, we see, among other things, that Jesus came to do something for us which is of utmost importance. Listen: "If the blood of bulls and of goats, and the ashes of an heifer sprinkling the unclean, sanctifieth to the purifying of the flesh, how much more shall the blood of Christ, who through the eternal Spirit offered Himself without spot to God, purge your conscience from dead works."

What the writer wants to say to you and to me this morning is this: God used a variety of rituals and forms to teach great spiritual truths to His people in the Old Covenant. He taught them that if they would touch certain things, they would become unclean. This was to remind them over and over that they were stained with sin. Then He directed them to present certain sacrifices in the Temple. If they presented these sacrifices and were touched by the ashes of the sacrifices, they were again made ceremonially clean. This was to teach them that one day a Messiah would come who would be sacrificed for them. When this happened, then they should be cleansed of all their sins.

If you and I want to understand properly what this Messiah did for us, then we must not conceive of Him merely as One who redeemed us from our sins so that we can get into heaven, but we must think of Him as One who has purged our consciences from dead works. And, oh, what a tremendous blessing that is!

Not so long ago human beings in general did not pay too much attention to the importance of conscience. Christians have always had their consciences instructed. They have been taught to listen to the voice of conscience and have learned something of its significance. But individuals who were not instructed and who stood on the outside had the notion that conscience should not be respected by one who is a man.

Today they are learning better. The modern psychologist knows that such a view of conscience is altogether wrong.

Conscience plays a tremendous part in human life. If a person has a bad conscience, if there is something inside him which is accusing him, this has its repercussions in his whole life.

LOVE DRIVES OUT FEAR

First of all, it introduces fear. A person with a bad conscience is always being haunted by fear. It is not merely a matter of form when a gunman sleeps with a gun under his pillow. That is a manifestation of fear. By day and by night, no matter whether he is in the company of people whom he regards as his friends or not, he is always afraid because he has a bad conscience. So it is.—What plays a more devastating part in the lives of human beings than fear? Think how happy you and I would be if we never had fears. The reason why we worry so much, why we are so consumed by anxiety about tomorrow, why we are so concerned about our health, our jobs, our business, old age, and so on, is that we are not altogether clean in our relationship between God and ourselves. If we were sure of that; if we could always steadily look God in the eye; if we would just cast ourselves without one bit of fear or hesitancy completely upon the mercies of God, fear would be gone, for "perfect love casteth out fear."

JESUS PURGES OUR CONSCIENCES

So when Jesus came to take our sins away, He came to purge our consciences. He doesn't want us to be haunted by demons of fear as we make our way through this world. He wants joy to be in our hearts, and assurance and strength, so that we can face each new day with a clean conscience not because we think we are so correct, but because we know, because we are sure, that the love of God is with us. So you see, the religion of Jesus and His redeeming love is not only something for death. No, it is a very real thing for life, for now, because it purges our consciences.

Well, this matter of conscience has another significance. If I have boys or girls in my confirmation class who are sulking and who manifest an ugly mood or temper, they need not tell me any more. I know they have a bad conscience. They have done something they should not have done. Because they have a bad conscience, they have to behave as they behave. That is true not only of the children in the confirmation class, that is true of children all over the world, and in this respect we are all children. It is true of everyone. Many a man comes home and is terribly abusive to his wife and to his children because he has a bad conscience. He is on the defensive. Many a woman heaps scorn and abuse upon her husband because she has a bad conscience. She is on the defensive. This goes all through life. A bad conscience has a very evil influence on human conduct.

But now Jesus is come. He gave Himself on Calvary. Why? Well, to take away the things because of which we have a bad conscience. He came to remove our sins so that we should find peace with God, so that our hearts should be at ease and our souls should be relieved, so that a heavenly peace can come in and take up its abode within us. If we can have our consciences purged; if we can stand easily in the presence of God; if instead of trying to hide away from our Creator we can look up to God because we are covered with the holiness of our Savior's garment of righteousness, well, that is a different matter. Then we need no longer be on the defensive. Then we can be frank and free and happy in our relationship to our fellow men. We need not try to conceal and hide the things for which we feel guilty in our hearts and souls. So you see that when Jesus came, He did not try to do something which has relationship only to eternity. No, He came to do something which is basic for our life here and now. He came to purge our consciences.

NEW STRENGTH FOR LIFE

But even that is not all. The holy writer says: "How much more shall the blood of Christ, who through the eternal Spirit offered Himself without spot to God, purge your conscience from dead works to serve the living God?" Martin Luther had a clear understanding of this particular truth, and he expressed it adequately, in a manner which has enjoyed universal admiration ever since he penned these words. As a matter of fact, these words have been called the most significant single-sentence statement ever penned by the hand of uninspired mortal man: "I believe that Jesus Christ, true God, begotten of the Father from eternity, and also true man, born of the Virgin Mary, is my Lord, who has redeemed me, a lost and condemned creature, purchased and won me from all sins, from death, and from the power of the devil; not with gold or silver, but with His holy precious blood and with His innocent suffering and death, that I may be His own and live under Him in His kingdom and serve Him in everlasting righteousness, innocence, and blessedness." You see, Jesus did not come to redeem us only for eternity. Jesus came to redeem us for a life that is to be lived now, "to serve the living God."

The individual who stands before the Cross of Christ and who realizes that the Son of God became man, so to suffer and die that he might live, finds himself in a special relationship of grateful indebtedness to this Christ. In life the important thing is not always *what* you do, but *why* you do what you do. Sometimes what you do will not be impressive, and yet the reason why you do it may be very, very beautiful and noble. Jesus sat in the Temple one day. He watched people putting gifts into the Temple treasury. Some gave very sizable gifts, but among the givers was a poor widow. She gave not only *something*, but she gave *everything* she had. It was very little. Whether it was given or was not given would not make very much difference in the operation of the Temple, but she gave with her whole heart.

A little child comes to our kindergarten, and the teacher teaches it to make something for Mother's Day. It is not even worth a penny in actual monetary value, but when it reaches the mother's hand and the mother realizes that behind this little scrawl and this little drawing is the heart of this little child, then this little thing becomes a very precious gift, not because of the monetary value, but because of the *why* that is behind this gift. And so it is in the life of the Christian.

DYNAMIC OF LOVE

When the Christian learns that he is redeemed by the blood of Jesus Christ, that becomes the *why* behind his acts. All the things he does, he does because he loves this Christ. He loves because Christ first loved him. And so life becomes an adventure in the expression of love and of gratitude. You see, that is the nerve of purpose and spirit that lies behind the living of a Christian life. It was for this Jesus redeemed us. Had Jesus not redeemed us, we should be in the power of sin. Our hearts would be selfish and self-centered, and we should know nothing of this love and gratitude, which seeks no personal gain, but merely desires to express love and appreciation.

Life moves to higher levels when you begin to live it from such motives. Christianity is to preserve you from a miserable existence. It is to keep you from the sordid spirit of money grabbing. It is to keep you from becoming a slave who is enchained in lust and sin. The love of Jesus revealed and expressed for you on Calvary has removed the burden of sin and made you free so that, liberated from these chains, you now can, in grateful loving service, give your life to your fellow men because Jesus first gave Himself for you. So Christianity is not just a religion for death. It is a religion for life, for now. It provides the essence for really beautiful, noble, and victorious living. There is no use making nice words about freedom of spirit, about conscience, about freedom of soul, unless Christ is in the picture, for only He and His redemptive work can provide what is needed for such freedom and happiness.

FOR DEATH

But the religion of Jesus is not only for this life. It meets the basic necessities of life, but it goes beyond that. It also is a religion for death and for eternity. No man really can be happy unless he knows he has the satisfying answer to the question of death. It does not make any difference who you are and how richly you may have been endowed with gifts of mind and artistic skills or material possessions—if you know that each tick of the clock is bringing you closer to that day when you must leave all these earthly things behind and you do not know what lies beyond, then you cannot be happy in the enjoyment of this world's blessings. Whatever you have will always be marred by the worries about that which lies ahead. No matter how brightly the sun would like to shine in your life, there will always be that dark cloud of gloom which will obscure that light. It is not until you have found the answer to death and to eternity that you can be truly a happy member of God's family.

If we understand what Jesus accomplished for us by His redemptive work, then we know that He provides the answer to this question. Listen: "But Christ being come an High

Priest of good things to come, by a greater and more perfect tabernacle, not made with hands, that is to say, not of this building; neither by the blood of goats and calves, but by His own blood He entered in once into the Holy Place, having obtained eternal redemption for us." Or listen to this: "And for this cause He is the Mediator of the new testament, that by means of death, for the redemption of the transgressions that were under the first testament, they which are called might receive the promise of eternal inheritance." There is your answer. Jesus did not only die to bring us things for this life, but He died also to take from us all fear of death and insure for us an eternal inheritance and everlasting life.

GLORY OF HEAVEN

Various people have various ideas about eternity and about heaven. The Mohammedans have pictured heaven to themselves in very sensual terms. They think of heaven as a place where all the human appetites will be satisfied. But the Holy Scriptures give us a different picture. The Holy Scriptures give us a heaven which is designed to satisfy our souls and which gives us a happiness which we cannot even comprehend in this life and world.

The Bible sometimes speaks of heaven as a beautiful city. Then again it speaks of heaven as being in the presence of God, being right with your Father in all His divine majesty and glory, having the happiness of a child who has come home. Then it speaks of heaven as an existence where there is fullness of joy and where there are pleasures forevermore. Then it speaks of heaven as being at the great wedding feast of the Lamb, where all tears are wiped away. So the Bible holds out to us a beautiful picture.

And I assure you that it is the answer. I have seen more

than one person die, and I have seen them die clapping their hands with joy, absolutely sure that when they close their eyes on this world, they will step into the joy which Jesus has gone to prepare.

So you see, Christianity is beautiful. It has meaning not only for eternity, but for now. It has meaning not only for now, but also for eternity. Life may pose many practical problems. Many irritating issues may come up, and we may scratch our head and trouble ourselves a great deal, wondering how we are going to find the practical solutions to this problem and that. But, my friends, nothing can break you when you have the solid foundation. Then you can weather every storm. Then you will be the victor, and even death will be overcome.

May the Spirit of God give to us a really full and adequate appreciation and understanding of the redeeming love of God in Christ Jesus, our Mediator. Amen.

The Christian Faith

❖ ❖ ❖

*Let this mind be in you which was also in Christ Jesus, who, being in the form of God, thought it not robbery to be equal with God, but made Himself of no reputation and took upon Him the form of a servant and was made in the likeness of men. And being found in fashion as a man, He humbled Himself and became obedient unto death, even the death of the Cross. Wherefore God also hath highly exalted Him and given Him a name which is above every name, that at the name of Jesus every knee should bow, of things in heaven and things in earth and things under the earth, and that every tongue should confess that Jesus Christ is Lord, to the glory of God the Father.—*PHILIPPIANS *2:5-11.*

Nineteen hundred odd years ago this day, Jesus, our blessed Lord, rode triumphantly into the city of Jerusalem. He was acclaimed by great multitudes of people, as we are told in the Gospel for today. They hailed Him as the One who came in the name of the Lord. They sang their happy hosannas and called Him David's royal Son. To this day, children of God regard this as the favorite day on which to have those who have found their Savior make a declaration of faith and profess Him before all the world. And so we also have the pleasure of again having in our service on this Palm Sunday a happy group of older and younger Christians who want to say to the world that they believe the truths of God. Even as men professed their faith when Jesus came into Jerusalem, so do the children of God still proclaim their faith.

LORDS MANY

The heart of this faith, which embraces a number of very important truths, the very heart and core of this faith, is expressed in the words of our text which say: "Every tongue should confess that Jesus Christ is Lord."

Human beings the world round have their respective faiths. People have all through the ages professed their faith in lords many and in gods many. This is still true. Some of our day, millions of them, profess their faith in Allah. Many other millions profess their faith in the gods of Hinduism. You and I have had abundant opportunity to read in recent months how these millions, holding to opposing faiths, have been fighting against one another and turning the land of India into a sea of blood, as it were.

Many acknowledge reason to be their lord. They believe that reason is capable of providing the answer for all the questions of life and that beyond the goddess of reason they need worship no one. Others worship pleasure as their lord. Whatever they think will bring pleasure into their lives is the dominant consideration so far as they are concerned.

We are witnessing in our day the sad spectacle of having literally tens and hundreds of millions of people recognize a man as their lord. Whatever his dictates, they obey them no matter in which country they find themselves or what their situation. For him they are ready to fight and die, to lie, to steal, to betray, to kill—whatever his orders may call for. So you see there are lords many and gods many whom people have followed through the ages and still follow. But they who are the sons and daughters of God know a different kind of Lord.

They say, "Jesus is the Lord." And they have good reason for saying it. They say, "Jesus is the Lord—their Savior," because that is what He came to be for them in this world. You and I as believing children of God accept Jesus as the only-begotten Son of the Father, who became man and who as man humbled Himself. He did not, as did the Romans of His day, make a spectacle of His power. Jesus, though He was the Son of God, did not display His divine splendor and glory. He lived with men as a man. He hungered. He thirsted. He sorrowed. He wept.

When the days of His public ministry were about completed and His teaching processes ended for that moment, and He was about to enter upon His great Passion, He went to Jerusalem. Masses acclaimed Him, but not for long. Soon they found Him to be the suffering Servant of Jehovah. He was under the olive trees in Gethsemane, sweating blood as He wrestled with the forces of hell. He was betrayed with a kiss. He was bound like a common prisoner and led away in shame and humiliation. He was placed before a variety of courts, which dealt with Him in most brutal fashion. He was struck in the face. He was scourged. He was spit upon. He was crowned with thorns and then innocently condemned to die; not only to die, but to die on the Cross—which was the most shameful way in which anyone could die in that day. Then, struggling along under the burden of that Cross, He stumblingly and tremblingly made His way to the top of Calvary. There they nailed Him to the accursed tree—a spectacle exposed to the scorn and contempt of godless, brutal men and women, who hissed at Him, who mocked Him and ridiculed Him even as He drew His dying breath. Deep down in His own soul He experienced what all the men of all times, lost in sin, should have experienced throughout eternity. He suffered the very pangs of hell as He cried out: "My God, My God, why hast Thou forsaken Me?" He gave Himself, humbled Himself even unto death, yea, the death of the Cross. And all of this He did because He had come to be "the Lamb of God, which taketh away the sin of the world."

When He had breathed His last and the executioners were sure of His passing, friends took Him from the Cross, wrapped His body in graveclothes, and placed Him into Joseph's tomb. Had He, or had He not, succeeded in overcoming the powers of evil? The third day He provided the evidence. He arose from the dead. Then men could know. He was delivered for our offenses, but He was raised again for our justification. The work of redemption was a completed fact. And from that time to this there have been those who have called Him Lord. Peter said, as he made his confession: "Thou art the Christ, the Son of the living God." Thomas, when he saw his living, resurrected Lord, said: "My Lord and my God." Martin Luther fifteen hundred years later said: "That is my Lord, who has redeemed me, a lost and condemned creature." And that, my friends, is the confession of God's children everywhere: "Jesus Christ is the Lord, who has saved us from our sins."

JESUS IS LORD OF LORDS

Christians, however, think of Jesus not only as the Lord who has saved them, but also as the Lord of Lords and the King of Kings. Our text says, "God also hath highly exalted Him and given Him a name which is above every name."

Nothing could have looked more hopeless than the case and cause of Christ when He was dying on the Cross. And yet, this One, who gave Himself for the sins of men, forty days after His resurrection, ascended on high to sit at the right hand of the Father. All who believe in Him go through life with a certain strength and confidence in their hearts, because they know the government of the universe is held in the hand of their Brother, the God-Man, who loves them with an unfailing love. They know that His is an infinite power and that He finally controls all things.

It is this which inspires Christians with the assured hope that the Church of God shall never perish. Many enemies have tried to destroy it. They have tried to wipe Jesus out as the Savior, as the Lord of Lords and King of Kings. The attacks upon Jesus were made very early in the Christian movement. They have continued to be made down to our own generation. There has never been a day from that time till now in which there were not some people aggressively attacking Christ.

They have also tried to destroy the Church. Men have stopped short of no cruelties and brutalities which the sinful heart of men could devise in their effort to stamp out Christianity. The Romans burned the early Christians like so many torches. They threw them to the lions. They robbed them of their possessions and of their children, only to discover that the blood of the martyrs became the seed of the Church. Jesus had said that the gates of hell shall not prevail against His Church, and so they have not. Men have tried by cunning, by bitterness, by contempt, by sneers and leers, to do away with Christianity. We in our own time have witnessed some of the most terrific and diabolical efforts that have ever been made to destroy the Church. The concentration camps of Nazi Germany, the persecutions of Communistic Russia, the bitterness and hatred of unbelievers and atheists in every country of the world, have been directed to the destruction of the Church of Jesus Christ. Yet, I think, we can say today with hearts that overflow with joy and gratitude to Almighty God that there has been no generation of people in many centuries, if ever before, in the history of the world which has had the privilege of witnessing such a mighty resurgence of Christianity as is true in this very hour. All over our own country there is an interest in the truths of God such as has not existed within the time and memory of any living man. It's one of the really encouraging and thrilling things, to be able to see how more and more people are becoming concerned about this.

Only yesterday I happened to sit in a group of men not of our Church, and they turned to me, and they said: "What do you think about the decision of the Supreme Court of the United States with reference to the teaching of religion in public schools?" Thus began a bit of a discussion. Though the men sitting to my right and to my left belonged to churches which had done very, very little for the religious training of the youth, they were agreed that maybe the decision of the Court would be a blessing in disguise because it would make churches realize as they had not realized for a long time what their obligations are over against the young in their parishes and in the communities in which their churches are seeking to serve the souls of men.

My friends, there is an interest. We could not begin to give you even a brief account of all these manifestations of a revival of interest in the Gospel of Jesus Christ. The other evening when we had our meeting of the Men's Club, one of our men turned to me and said: "I just heard them say over the radio as I drove home this evening from work that there are great Christian revivals going on over in Japan and that any day now it might well happen that the Emperor of Japan will profess himself to be a Christian." Over in Europe, in India, in China, in Japan, the islands of the sea, literally everywhere, growing numbers of men and women, boys and girls, are reaching up and taking hold of that Cross. As they look into the face of Jesus, they are saying: "That is my Lord, who has redeemed me."

Christians, who believe in this Lord, believe in Him not only as One who can preserve His Church, but also as the Lord of Lords, who is in control of all human affairs. They know that they have a responsibility. They know that God has given them minds and powers which they are to exercise for the good of human society. God realizes full well how great are the terrific forces of evil in this world, and Christians know how determined these forces are to destroy man, God's most wonderful visible creature. But Christians also believe that in the final analysis all of the plotting and the scheming and the machinations of the devil and all his cohorts shall not suffice to destroy the plans and purposes of God. They are sure that God hath exalted Jesus, that He hath put Him at His right hand, that He holds in His hands the control, the reins of the universe, and that one day all tongues must acknowledge Him to be the Lord. If they will not do so in the spirit of love and faith, they must do so as those whose necks have been bent before the overwhelming power of the almighty Lord. The confession of all Christians, then, is, "Jesus Christ is Lord."

DEVOTION TO CHRIST THE LORD

Because the children of God make this confession, therefore they have toward Him a sense of love and deepest gratitude. Contrary to popular opinion, Christians are the kind of people who know that they are not good. Some folks think

Christians are people who regard themselves as good. The truth is, of course, the other way around. Christians know that they are not good. That is why they come as humble sinners to Christ and trust in Him as the One who has taken their sins away. Because Christians stand before Jesus and believe in Him as the One who has died for them, that is why they feel toward Him an altogether inexpressible sense of love and gratitude. They don't want to hurt a Christ who has done for them what He has done. And so their life becomes an ongoing effort to pour out their love to Jesus by doing the things that will please Him.

So when people acknowledge Jesus as their Lord, they therewith also commit themselves to a way of life. They strive in all their conduct, in their thoughts, their words, their deeds, their feelings, to do as Jesus did. This applies not only to moral behavior in general, but it applies to every specific situation in life.

First of all, it applies to the behavior of the Christian in his own home. If you are going to show love to Jesus because of the things He has done for you, you must start at home. That is where He puts the very first people before you over against whom you can show your gratitude. If you don't show love to the people in your own home, there's no use talking about faith in Jesus or about having love in your heart.

Then the Lord provides us our next opportunity for showing love through the fellow men with whom we work. Whether we are the employer or employee, or whether we happen to be people in one or another profession, it all matters not — we must all work with somebody; and the people with whom we work afford us the next chance in life to show our love.

Then God gives us a place in human society as citizens, in

the community, the State, the nation. And there, in our civic relationships, He gives us the next opportunity to show our love. And so all through life, wherever we find ourselves, God is placing opportunities in our way, through the acceptance of which we can give expression to the fact that we love because He first loved us.

SHARE GOSPEL

One of the greatest of all responsibilities which the Lord has laid upon our hearts is that of sharing with our fellow men the knowledge of salvation. Whenever another soul has come to stand on Calvary and to see Jesus as Lord and Savior, there goes with that blessed experience the immediate obligation to carry that revelation to others who have not yet learned to know the Gospel of Jesus Christ.

If it be true that the world is in a state of confusion and chaos this morning; if there are hundreds of millions of people who are looking either to Mohammed, or the gods of Hinduism, or a Stalin, or to some other kind of idol as their lord, then it is our holy obligation to do what we can to hold up the light of the Gospel, so that it can throw its penetrating rays into this darkness of idolatry, paganism, and sin, and thus illumine the hearts of others as our hearts have been illuminated by the enlightening influence of the Divine Spirit through the Gospel of Christ. We have an opportunity, a privilege, an obligation, such as has never before come to any generation of Christians. I say this not because we are the first Christians to whom God gave the command to preach the Gospel to all the world, but because we are living in a day in which the world has become much smaller than it has ever before been and in which people around the globe can be reached more speedily, more cheaply, more effectively, than has ever before been true. So our Lord's command to go and preach, to go and share, could never have quite meant to others what it should mean to us.

Well, my friends, all of this is important for each one of us, but it takes on special significance when we consider the fact that before me we have two dozen boys and girls and as many men and women who are here to declare their faith, to say to all the world and to you: "We believe in the true God and in Jesus as the Lord, whom He sent to be our Savior, and we want to dedicate our lives to His service."

For this each of us must breathe a prayer of thanksgiving to the heavenly Father and to the Spirit of God, who alone can work faith in the hearts of men, whether they be old or whether they be young. It is a wonderful thing so to declare one's faith, and a grand privilege, but, my friends, the fact that it carries with it a consecration to a way of life makes it difficult. To be a Christian never in history has been easy, and never will be.

WE ARE WEAK

The Apostle Paul found that out. He found it out first of all in himself. That's why he said: "The good that I would, I do not; but the evil, which I would not, that I do." He found it out in the people who had joined him as converts and then became untrue to their professions of faith and returned to the world, from which they had come. Jesus found it out. He was tempted in all points like as we are, and it occasioned even for Him a terrific struggle. Jesus also found it out in His ministry. There were those who followed Him for a time, but then they abandoned Him again and went back to the world. Jesus got the most heartbreaking evidence for this on the night when one of the men who had professed to be His disciple came up and kissed Him and thus by a kiss for thirty paltry pieces of silver sold Him into the hands of His enemies. You see, to profess faith in the true God and to vow loyalty to Christ for life is not something to be done lightly or to be accepted as a vow that can be kept easily.

We want you to know that on our own part we are struggling, seeking to remain true to God as He provides the strength. We want you to know that our prayers ascend to God's throne of grace in your behalf that you may be strong. It is at this point, you see, where the use of the divine means of grace enters in. Some people have an idea that once they have learned the way of salvation, they need not bother about it any more. The truth is they really haven't learned it, at least not in all of its practical implications, if they so think. And they certainly have not learned anything about the subtleness of evil. No, God has given us the Bread of Life, in His holy Word, in the beautiful Sacrament, so that regularly and faithfully we may eat of that bread and drink of that cup and thus be strengthened and refreshed and given new ability to walk in the pathways of God.

What is true for those who are making a profession of their faith today is true of all of us. Our Lord said: "Not everyone that saith unto Me, Lord, Lord, shall enter into the kingdom of heaven; but he that doeth the will of My Father which is in heaven." Our text says we should be minded as Jesus was and give our lives in love and humility. Our Savior warned: "Blessed are they that hear the Word of God and keep it." And the final book of the Scriptures calls out to everyone who claims Jesus as his Lord: "Be thou faithful unto death, and I will give thee a crown of life."

May it please the Spirit of God, who has brought us to

know Jesus as our Lord, to help us be true unto Him, so that one day, having lived richly and victoriously in this world for the glory of God and for the good of our fellow men, we may hear from the lips of our blessed Savior those beautiful words: "Well done, thou good and faithful servant."

Jesus Is Risen

❖   ❖   ❖

Now, if Christ be preached that He rose from the dead, how say some among you that there is no resurrection of the dead? But if there be no resurrection of the dead, then is Christ not risen. And if Christ be not risen, then is our preaching vain, and your faith is also vain. Yea, and we are found false witnesses of God, because we have testified of God that He raised up Christ, whom He raised not up if so be that the dead rise not. For if the dead rise not, then is not Christ raised. And if Christ be not raised, your faith is vain; ye are yet in your sins. Then they also which are fallen asleep in Christ are perished. If in this life only we have hope in Christ, we are of all men most miserable. But now is Christ risen from the dead and become the First Fruits of them that slept.—I CORINTHIANS 15:12-20.

May it please God, in His infinite mercy, to let every moment of this beautiful day be a blessing to us and to countless other men in all parts of the world, as the message of our risen Lord once again is heard to bring men to faith, to strengthen men in faith, to give them hope and courage for the day that lies ahead, for Jesus' sake. Amen.

THE FACT OF THE RESURRECTION

Christ the Lord is risen today. That is the glorious fact which we, together with all other Christians, commemorate

on Easter Sunday. This, praise God, is a fact! Jesus is risen.
Our Lord had brought His great work of redemption to its
climax on Calvary. Without shrinking from even its most
painful aspects, He had borne the total guilt of the human
family. He had suffered indignity and shame. He had
stretched out His arms on the accursed tree. He had endured
the full anguish and agony of hell. He had given His last
sigh, His last drop of blood. When He had gasped out life,
He was taken from the Cross by friends, who wrapped Him
in graveclothes and placed Him into Joseph's tomb. The
work of redemption was completed.

Jesus had said, "It is finished," but it yet remained for
Him to deliver the evidence for this fact. So on the third day
after His death on Calvary, He came out of the tomb, the
living, victorious Christ, who had burst the bonds of death
and who for time and for eternity had established Himself as
the Victor over the enemies of men's immortal souls.

Men who hated Him in that day, some 1,900 years ago,
refused to admit that Jesus had risen. In their own bungling,
blundering way they tried to deny the reality of Christ's
resurrection. Twenty years later, when Paul was preaching
this story of Jesus on Mount Areopagus to the philosophers
of Athens, at least some of them just laughed in his face. They
wouldn't believe that Jesus had come back from the dead.
And to this day there are people who deny that Jesus arose.
They will acknowledge that if you put a kernel of wheat into
the ground, it will disintegrate, and yet out of that dying,
disintegrating seed will come a new plant, bearing scores of
new seeds. They will admit that the ugliest of lily bulbs
planted into the ground will disintegrate, and yet out of it
will come a beautiful plant, bearing lovely flowers. This they
must acknowledge to be a fact. And yet, while they grant
that a little kernel of wheat can rise, that an ugly lily bulb

can spring into a new life, they will stubbornly insist that it could not have happened to the Son of God.

My friends, whatever the enemies of Jesus may have said to the contrary in the past, or yet may say in time that lies before us, the facts are these. God has prophesied that Jesus would arise. The holy writer had said, "Thou wilt not suffer Thine Holy One to see corruption." God had even symbolized the resurrection of Jesus through the experiences of a Jonah. Jesus Himself had asserted, "Destroy this temple, and in three days I will raise it up."

What God had promised, what Jesus had foretold, came to pass. It was an angel of God who said to the amazed women: "Why seek ye the living among the dead? He is not here. He is risen." Jesus appeared to His disciples. Though they had to pay with their own lifeblood for the un- yielding insistence that Jesus arose and lived, yet they had seen Him, they had heard Him. How could they deny what they knew to be a reality? And so one after another went down to a martyr's death rather than to contradict what they knew to be the most glorious of all historic facts: Christ the Lord is risen.

THE RESURRECTION VALIDATES CHRIST'S CLAIMS

Whatever men may do about it, whatever their attitudes toward it may be, it will all not change the stubborn fact. Jesus is the living Lord. The Spirit of God points out else- where that this resurrection of Jesus declares Him to be the Son of God. "He is declared to be the Son of God with power," say the Scriptures, "by the resurrection from the dead." The resurrection of Jesus validates His every claim. He had placed Himself before men not merely as the Son of Mary, but also as the Son of God. He had said, "The Father and I are one." What He did had not merely the relative value which the deeds of a human might have, but the infinite value of One who was the Son of God Himself.

The resurrection of Jesus, as Christians have been quick to perceive, also has given meaning to every promise received from the lips of Christ. Our Lord, during the days of His public ministry, gave many beautiful promises. As a matter of fact, this holy Book is filled with promises which have meaning for you. These promises would not be of much value had Jesus not kept His promise to arise. He had said: "Destroy this temple, and in three days I will raise it up." There lay the test. If He could not keep that promise, His followers and disciples in the centuries to come would look in vain to Him for a fulfillment of any other promise. But He kept the promise and thus has given support and meaning to every promise He has ever made. If He said to you: "Lo, I am with you alway, even unto the end of the world," you need never again feel lonely. You need never again be afraid, because you know that promise stands. If He reaches out His hands toward you and says to you: "Come unto Me, all ye that labor and are heavy laden, and I will give you rest," those are not just empty words. They have meaning and value because they are the promise of Jesus. If Jesus says to you: "Him that cometh to Me I will in no wise cast out," take His promise at its face value, for He means what He says, and He intends to keep what He has promised.

THE RESURRECTION ASSURES OUR REDEMPTION

Paul, in the words of our text, points out specifically that this resurrection of Jesus, this great and glorious fact, the most glorious in all history, is to us an assurance that we now are the redeemed of God. Paul puts it in an argumentative way. Approaching it somewhat negatively, he forces the reader of His words to come with him to the conclusion that there is only one possible meaning and significance, and that is, that now since Christ arose, we are no longer in our sins.

The suffering of Jesus was not a meaningless suffering. It was not, like the Greek tragedy, something in which the hero became involved contrary to his will. The suffering and the dying of Jesus was according to divine plan. It was the outpouring of divine love for the sake of effecting the salvation of the whole human family. Jesus came not to be a meaningless hero, but to be the Savior of men. He said: "The Son of Man is come to seek and to save that which was lost." He told His disciples the Son of Man must go to Jerusalem and suffer and die in order to accomplish His purpose.

Jesus had gone. He had given His life. All seemed to be hanging in the balance. Men wondered what the outcome of it all might be. But when He arose, there was no further room for questioning. That was the answer. Now the faith of those who believed in Him could no longer be in vain. They should be sure they were redeemed. Paul gives such emphasis to this fact, and he could do so as a matter of personal conviction because he had experienced in his own heart just what that meant.

PAUL FOUND PEACE

There was a time when Paul didn't have the assurance of forgiveness. He had a conviction of guilt. His sensitive conscience told him that he didn't do what he ought to do, that he was in trouble with his Maker. But he never succeeded in satisfying the demands of God. No matter how he tried, he was certain that he was always falling short of the perfect requirements of God. But now, one day, God allowed him to see Jesus, the risen Lord, the One who had come to die for men so as to save them from their sins. Paul had seen Him. Now something happened in the heart of Paul. He gained an assurance which he had never before possessed. For the first time in his life his heart was filled with the spirit of joy, and he was genuinely at ease. Up to that time he had to admit that the Law was condemning him, that he was dying under it day by day. But now there came into his heart a sense of peace, the assurance of well-being in his relationship to God. He knew that there was a perfect reconciliation between the Father, whom he had offended, and himself, the offender.

GOD IS FOR US

This joy which Paul experienced when he became assured that his sins had been atoned for should be the joy of every individual who finds Christ. You must have experienced in your life many times what it means to become fearful. Surely you have had your moments when you worried and wondered. Perhaps you jump when you see the lightning flash or hear the thunder crash. Perhaps even a little sudden noise shocks you, gives you a chill. We are terrified human beings. The reason why we are so filled with terror, why the clouds of fear and gloom hang over us, is that within our hearts there is a consciousness of sin. If you and I knew that all was well between God and us, we shouldn't be afraid. Nothing in this world could terrify us. And it is this, this sweet, wonderful peace, which Easter should bring to our hearts. The resurrection of Jesus should be to you the assurance that God does not count your sins against you because they were counted against Christ and He paid for them. His resurrection is the assurance that He completed His task. You shouldn't be driven to despair and distraction by inner fears, tensions. You should be a happy son or daughter of God in Christ.

CHRIST'S RESURRECTION GIVES POWER OVER SIN

Paul knew from personal experience that the resurrection of Jesus gave him not only the assurance of having been redeemed from the guilt of sin, but also the knowledge that Jesus had freed him from the power of sin. Paul had done a lot of things in his life because of which he was unspeakably ashamed. The one thing which bothered him more than all else was the fact that one day he had stood by and watched while the enemies stoned Stephen, the first Christian martyr, to death. Paul had stood by and given his consent to this terrible, murderous deed. He had been proud, haughty, cruel. He had persecuted the Christians. He had tried to destroy Christianity in its very infancy. The things he had done had been blasphemous and awful. He knew that. Paul also knew that as he struggled on through life, it was exceedingly difficult to do the things that would please God. Even when he was in the advanced years of his Apostolic ministry, he still was not doing things perfectly. That's why he said: "The things I would, I do not, and the things I would not, I do." "The spirit is willing, but the flesh is weak." And yet, out of the resurrection of Jesus had come an assurance that he, like all others, was to be free from the power of sin. No longer was he the helpless, hopeless victim of the forces of evil. Now the love of Jesus had come into his heart. It had become the driving, impelling motive of his life. Because Jesus had suffered for him, risen for him, Jesus was the Lord and Master of his soul. That is why each day he dedicated and rededicated himself to the one task of doing the things that would please this Christ. And so he learned from what the Spirit of

God did in him and for him how wonderful were the fruits and the results of Christ's resurrection.

CHRIST'S RESURRECTION FREES FROM DEATH

But sweetest of all was the fact that Jesus had redeemed not only from the guilt and the power of sin, but also from the tragic consequences of sin. God had said: "The wages of sin is death." "The soul that sinneth it shall die." This was Paul's problem as well as the problem of all other human beings. But now Jesus had come. He had borne the punishment which men should have endured. He had died, One for all. Because He had come out of that tomb and death lay conquered under the Hero's heel, Paul could rejoice with such a full heart. He knew that now Jesus had become the First Fruits among them that sleep. Even as Jesus arose, so each individual who believed in Christ should with Christ and through Christ rise unto a new life. Death was overcome.

This, my friends, has its meaning. The resurrection of Jesus should not only afford us peace of heart and give us the inner joyful confidence that we can, by the power of God, learn to live more like the sons and daughters of God with each passing day, but the resurrection of Jesus should also give us the answer to the last great problem, the problem of death.

Since we last celebrated Easter, some of you have had loved ones taken from your side. You have followed their lifeless bodies to their last earthly resting place. This is always one of the experiences of humans which affect them most profoundly. Oh, how we hate to give up our dear ones! What a painful experience it is to be separated from them! It would be stark, unrelieved tragedy indeed were it not for the resurrection of Jesus. But now, since He arose and became the First Fruits among them that sleep, His resurrection is an assurance that all who fall asleep in Christ shall rise unto life eternal. That is the beautiful truth which always has served from that time to this, and for all time to come shall serve, as an effective means to dry our tears, to cheer our hearts, to heal the bleeding wounds. When you know that your dear ones who have departed this life have gone to be with Christ, that they have been relieved from all of the terrifying experiences of this world, from all the heart-aches and griefs, the sorrows and the sufferings of time, from all the fearful consequences of sin which come also upon the children of God during their earthly pilgrimage, when you know that your dear ones have been freed from all of these things and that they have come to rest in God, then you can even through your tears thank Him for having taken them out of this vale of tears unto Himself. As we think of the gain which our loved ones who departed have experienced, we are able with greater courage to carry the loss which we have endured.

FIRST FRUITS

But even as our dear ones came to the end of life's road, so one day you and I, too, will be called. We do not know when. Only the other day I received a special-delivery air-mail letter from one of the men who was a roommate of mine at school. He wrote that his wife had suddenly passed away during the hours of the night. Right out of the midst of life, unexpectedly, without warning, men and women can be torn away by the cold, cruel hand of death. Death is no respecter of persons, whether it be the newborn child, whether it be the young person in the full power of life and vigor, whether it be the tired old pilgrim who has come into old age—death is no respecter of persons. But if you and I know that we have our champion in Christ, that death has been overcome, and that when the final call comes our way, it will only mean that we shall for a moment close our eyes upon the things of this world to open them again upon the indescribable glories of the heaven that awaits us, then you see we can live out each day in utter fearlessness. With calmness and strength we can go on our way because we know Jesus is the First Fruits among them that sleep.

My friends, may it please God in His infinite love and mercy to impress upon the hearts of each one of us the meaning of Easter, so that we in Christ will have the Savior, who has redeemed us from our sins, made it possible for us to fight against the power of evil, and given us the answer to the last and the greatest problem of all. May He to that end be with us for Jesus' sake. Amen.

Old Truths for a New Day

22 Sermons on the Old-Line Epistles

FROM ADVENT TO EASTER

VOLUME ONE

By O. A. GEISEMAN

Here is timely, powerful, persuasive preaching by one of America's pulpit masters.

Dr. Geiseman speaks from the fullness of real life experiences. He knows people, their problems, heartaches, temptations, strivings — and for each he has a personal word of exhortation and encouragement.

"How to Be Strong, Decisive, Victorious"; "How to Be Happy"; "A Cheerful Outlook"; "Is Christianity Worth the Price?"; "How to Overcome Evil"; "Are You Winning the Race of Life?" are some of the compelling themes treated in this inspiring new volume. Each message is a personal challenge to more sanctified, Christ-centered living.

Ministers who are looking for preaching at its best will find these twenty-two sermons on the Old-Line Epistles most stimulating reading. All will gain from these pages a clearer understanding of the teachings of Christ and will learn how to apply them more directly to their daily living.

CONCORDIA   PUBLISHING   HOUSE

SAINT   LOUIS   18,   MISSOURI

PRINTED IN U. S. A.

www.ingramcontent.com/pod-product-compliance
Lightning Source LLC
Chambersburg PA
CBHW020353100426
42812CB00001B/42

9 780758 618061